# GOLD·LEAF
# TECHNIQUES

# GOLD·LEAF
# TECHNIQUES

Third Edition by Kent H. Smith
from original by Raymond LeBlanc, rev. by Arthur Sarti

ST Publications
Cincinnati, Ohio

Published by ST Publications, 407 Gilbert Avenue, Cincinnati, Ohio 45202, U.S.A.
Phone: 513-421-2050

Library of Congress Catalog Card Number: 85-63630
ISBN: 0-911380-71-X
Printed in the United States of America.
Staff of ST Publications:

Publisher: Jerry R. Swormstedt
Project Director: George B. Harper
Project Editor: Monica Stone
Art Director: Carol L. Hayfer

Typesetting by Digi-Type Graphics and JR Typesetting.

# Dedication

To Ray LeBlanc, who first wrote this text; my father, Howard F. Smith, who inspired me to be a gilder; Ted Brunskill, who introduced me to many advanced techniques; the Letterheads, for rekindling an interest in gilding; and to the serious student, who will carry on the traditions of quality workmanship.

# Preface

This book has been written and revised by sign painters for sign painters. When first published in 1961, the original text filled a great void; although there was a definite market for gold-leaf sign work, there was no complete text available on the subject. In subsequent years, gold leaf signs were seldom sold, and only the older sign painters still practiced the technique. Now that the market for such work is experiencing a revival, I have revised the original text to bring it up to date, both in techniques and materials.

It is a task that I, as a third-generation signman, have been pleased to undertake. Many of the processes used to produce the finest gold-leaf work are the same as they have been for many years. My grandfather, a stonecutter, did some signs and gilding, as many did in those days. I started working in my father's shop when I was five and progressed in my apprenticeship with him from card writing and through all phases of the sign trade until I reached what had always been my goal, gilding. As a result of this apprenticeship, much of my knowledge comes from an earlier era, when gilded sign work was more popular. We had many customers for fine gold-leaf signs, and it was not long before I was doing much of the work.

In days gone by, gilders learned the trade through apprenticeship either in the formal union training ground or under an individual master craftsman. That this is no longer the case is of real concern to me. Before anyone can successfully learn gilding, his understanding of the basics of lettering and layout and his knowledge of paints and surfaces must be as if by second nature. While it may be possible for an individual to learn the processes from this text well enough to complete a gilded sign, he will not work profitably or with ease until he masters brush control and proper lettering techniques. This does not come from learning the basics in a class or under tutelage, but rather with practice. Most journeyman sign painters would agree that it takes a minimum of two to three years to become acquainted with technique well enough to be able to call oneself an accomplished sign painter (or sign writer, as some prefer to be called). It is for this reason that both the original text and this revised edition have been written for the experienced sign painter.

LeBlanc explained this reasoning in his preface to the first edition: "This is not a book for beginning sign painters. It is assumed throughout that the reader is already familiar with the production of brush lettering, that he understands layout, is familiar with ordinary sign shop procedures, and has proper respect for his tools and materials. No space has been devoted to these aspects of sign painting except in those connections peculiar to working with leaf. But where work with leaf is involved, I have assumed no familiarity whatever with this material and have set down sufficient detail for the novice to get started, and I have carried through to all the fine points. The reader will find that all the methods described are practical, and they have been simplified to the greatest extent consistent with good work."

What has been included here is a detailed explanation of how to prepare and execute a gold-leaf sign. To the novice the description may frequently seem overly complicated. Often the explanation is more complicated than the process itself: This is only because we have tried to make the work as easy to understand as possible. As LeBlanc stated, "I ask the reader not to mistake detailed explanation for complexity. For example, I might describe the operation of laying leaf on glass by saying, as an old-time textbook did, 'The leaf is lifted from the book with the gilding tip and transferred to the glass with neatness and dispatch' instead of taking up two pages to explain exactly *how* this is accomplished. In the course of several years' working with gold leaf, the expert learns to do a lot of *little things* that make the work easy, and, not knowing these, the novice flounders. Throughout the writing of the book, I analyzed my methods of working; I kept asking myself, 'Just *how* do I do this, and *why* do I do it in this particular way?' And I have written all of it down so as to make it easy for you, too. Now I don't expect you to remember all these little points from just one reading. I suggest that after completing a job you think back and pick out the operations which gave you trouble, then refer to the section of the book that applies, and you will likely pick up a minor point that had escaped you at the first reading."

LeBlanc spent much of his life specializing in gold-leaf work, and he wrote that he did not relish the prospect of being "one of the last of the gold men." He hoped, through his book, "to stimulate a little more interest in doing gold-leaf signs and doing them well and possibly to inspire a few to become *craftsmen*."

Quality in craftsmanship is equally as important as quality in material when you are working with gold leaf, which has always been the most highly esteemed sector of the sign trade. This is something that hasn't changed over the years; LeBlanc himself discussed the same subject in his preface to the original edition of this book:

"I came to Hartford, Conn., in 1926 and have been here ever since except for a few brief periods. It was here that I learned to do gold work. Hartford has been a good training ground. As far back as anyone can remember there have always been several top-notch gold men here, with whom the rest of us have tried to keep up, with the result that the standard of workmanship in Hartford has always been exceptionally high. In the field of glass gilding especially you will find in Hartford a variety of treatments and effects seldom seen even in the larger cities. Hartford has had, also, three nationally-known gold leaf manufacturers.

"While traveling around the country recently, I visited many cities in which gold leaf work seems to be a disappearing art. This is inexcusable. Gold leaf signs are as popular today as they ever were, and the work is profitable and highly respectable. If the demand isn't being supplied, it is the fault of the signmen. I suppose much of this absence of good gold work can be explained as a symptom of the common American disease of doing things the easy way...why get involved in the intricacies of gold leaf work if one can get by without it? I don't expect to make much of a dent in this manner of thinking where it exists. I can't picture myself in the role of a crusader."

The thoughts expressed by LeBlanc are as significant today as they were in the 1960s. Although the processes of gilding are somewhat involved, the variety for design, as well as the satisfaction one gets from doing this advanced style of work, is endless. However, selling gold leaf has become increasingly difficult with the advent of screen printing and computer-generated graphics, so some help in looking at gilding from a positive viewpoint is needed. One of the ways to keep gilding alive is to sell your jobs not as gold leaf, but as a custom variety of window or other types of signs. Most customers don't understand what gold leaf is, nor do they appreciate the work involved until they actually see it being done. Very fine work can be sold as just that, without mention of gold other than casually in the selling process. Many customers balk at the idea of the expense of gold, but can be brought around by explaining its advertising impact and the durability of a product that will never fade and will last forever if properly serviced. Much of this is brought out in the text.

Except for temporary work, a good rule to follow is to ask yourself if gold leaf could be used either as the main medium of a sign or as an enhancement to every job you sell. Design and color are limited only by one's imagination and background. Some time spent researching will inspire you to use gold more creatively. No attempt has been made to do more than introduce some types of antique methods, even though they might be applied to modern signs. Much of this information can be found in the old texts. Some of these have been reprinted lately, particularly those by Atkinson and Strong*.

I have updated this edition to include newer products unavailable in LeBlanc's time — as well as to give alternatives to products unfortunately no longer available. Brand names of products have changed and most certainly will continue to change in future years. *Product types, however, remain which give the best results.* An appendix listing the most current suppliers has been added to this edition, and it is

*Atkinson, Frank H. *Atkinson Sign Painting.* Reprinted from 1909 edition. Cincinnati: ST Publications, 1983.

Strong, Charles J. and L.S. *Strong's Book of Designs.* Reprinted from 1910 edition. Cincinnati: ST Publications, 1982.

suggested that keeping current is a mere matter of reading the trade magazines and testing new products as they become available.

My final suggestion to you is to use this text as a reference and source book as well as a course of study. Remember that each operation requires practice and that each step should be perfected before moving on to the next. Expect to repeat many steps a number of times and waste some material as your *tuition* to this course before you will be able to say *honestly* to yourself, "That step I can do well. Now on to the next one."

Kent H. Smith
Greeley, Colorado
January, 1986

# Contents

# 1 Materials

One hesitates to mention brand names of materials when writing a book for fear of being accused of commercial motives and because information of this kind becomes obsolete so soon. However, it is difficult to avoid mentioning them, since in this line of work the choice of materials is so important that one might say it is essential. Sign painters' most common inquiries are about materials and where to find them. Therefore brand names are included for those materials we, the authors, have found most satisfactory in our work, both within the text and in the appendix. The listing is necessarily limited to those which are readily available at the time of writing. Undoubtedly many readers will be using other products that are equally satisfactory. Where the brand name of a material is given, it should be made clear that the material is being recommended only for the specific use described, that a blanket endorsement of the product for all purposes is *not* being given, and that it is only the individual product and not necessarily the entire line that is being recommended.

We are in a period during which new materials are being introduced, new formulations for existing materials are being created, and old standbys are being taken off the market at such a rapid rate that keeping up with the changes is a major difficulty. Many of the newer materials are superior to the old, familiar ones in important respects, but they often have different working characteristics and may require a little patience and experimentation in learning to work with them. A good example of this is the *Chromatic Clear Overcoat Varnish*, which was spawned by automotive finishes. It takes some time to get used to the peculiarities of this product, but it is so superior to the average urethane or spar varnish in lasting ability and adhesion to glass and vehicle finishes that it is worthwhile to learn to manage it.

A particularly troublesome situation arises because of many manufacturers' practice of changing the formulation of a product without so indicating on the label. Sometimes the new formulation works better than the old, but very often the change makes the new material unsuitable for the particular application for which it had previously been used in sign work. Sign painters must be alert for such changes.

Because of the rapid changes in materials, readers are urged to experiment constantly with new materials. You should try to have at all times at least one substitute that will work for each of your important materials, so that if one suddenly disappears or is changed enough to make it unusable, you won't be forced into a frenzy of experimentation in order to keep going. You can do this not only by trying everything new that comes along, but also by experimenting with new uses for old familiar products. The latter is especially important, as well as is recognizing changes in the working characteristics every time you open a new batch of an old favorite.

Experimentation with materials must be done intelligently. A comparison of two products used under different conditions, as on two different jobs, is meaningless. The only kind of test that will yield valuable information is to use the new product alongside the old one under a variety of conditions. This is best done in the shop. For example, suppose we want to try a new varnish for mixing backing paint. In the shop, gild a small area on a scrap piece of glass using silver leaf, which imposes a more strenuous requirement on the backing paint than does gold leaf. Next we back up several letters, using our old mixture on a portion of each letter and the new material on the remainder. We note which works better in the brush. In ten minutes, we try cleaning off the leaf from around the first letter, scrubbing hard enough to make the paint chip. Which of the two materials chips first? Then we try brushing varnish over the backing to see if either of the two materials will resist being picked up. We repeat the test on another letter after twenty minutes and on a third letter after an hour, leaving one letter to remain until the next day. Get the idea? The little time spent in making such a series of tests will tell you more about the relative merits of the two materials than you would glean from weeks of normal use on jobs.

Durability of materials is much more difficult to determine, since such information is not forthcoming until the material in question has been in service for some time. Moreover, durability is affected by many factors that are not under the sign painter's control and that vary from job to job. Again, comparing the lasting ability of two materials used on two different jobs is not a reliable test; the two materials have to be tested on the same job. One possible way of accomplishing this without risk of embarrassment is to try the new material on an imprint or a period. When testing on the job, remember to keep records so that you will remember what you used and where and when you used it.

**Varieties of Leaf**

Leaf of all kinds is supplied in books containing 25 leaves. Twenty such books (500 leaves) constitute a pack, the unit by which leaf is sold at wholesale. Gold leaf always measures 3 3/8 inches square; silver leaf is usually 3 3/4 inches square; and aluminum and variegated leaf is 5 1/2 inches square. Palladium leaf is the same size as gold leaf.

One gold leaf manufacturer has furnished the figure .0000035 inches (3 1/2 millionths of an inch or about three hundred thousand leaves to an inch) for the thickness of gold leaf, a figure which, however, will vary widely between different brands. Another manufacturer simply refers to the thickness as being one-half that of a sheet of rice paper. Either way, some of the various brands will run as thin as half that figure and some will be twice as thick. Some brands with lesser quality control will vary a great deal within each book; even each leaf will vary in thickness, usually from center to the edges. Silver leaf is rated at .00001 inches, or about three times as thick as gold leaf.

**XX Gold (23-Karat)**

Also known as "deep" gold. This is the most important variety of gold; it is the principal type used for glass gilding, and almost the only type used on signboards, trucks and general surface gilding. Burnished gilding on glass is nearly always done with XX leaf. It is supplied in two kinds of books; as *loose leaf* (the leaves are loose between rouged paper) and *patent leaf* (the leaves are lightly attached to tissue sheets for use when gilding in the wind). XX gold is also supplied on rolls of various widths. Patent leaf and leaf in rolls are seldom used for glass gilding. Some sign painters regularly use roll gold (long strips available in rolls) for stripes and letter outlines in glass gilding, as it is possible to lay a strip of leaf two or three feet long in one operation. When using patent leaf for these purposes, the size crawls badly on the gold, there is poor adhesion to the glass, and the gild tends to be cloudy. Using patent gold is not recommended for water-size gilding.

Loose-leaf XX gold is supplied in two grades: (1) *glass gold*, the best quality especially selected for glass gilding (with water size), and (2) *surface quality* (for use with oil and varnish sizes), which is a little cheaper. Surface gold has small imperfections, but is satisfactory for all surface gilding applications. It is possible to use some brands of surface gold for glass gilding, although they may require more patching. Some experimentation is necessary to find the best grade to use from the brands available to you.

**Lemon Gold (18-Karat)**    This is supplied only in loose-leaf form, as it is used principally for glass gilding. However, lemon gold can be used on signboards and trucks if the work is varnished, and some novel effects are possible with lemon gold used in combination with XX gold on such surface applications. The principal use for lemon gold is in glass gilding, especially for matte centers with burnished XX gold outlines. Burnished gilding on glass can also be done with lemon gold and is particularly useful on lightly tinted glass, as the lemon gold is lighter in color and shows better through the tint.

**Pale Gold (16-Karat)**    Similar to lemon gold but even lighter in color, pale gold is used for the same purposes as lemon gold. Pale gold is sometimes called *white gold*, which is misleading, since it is not silvery in color but retains a pale yellow tint.

**White Gold (12-Karat)**    Also 13 1/2- and 14-karat in some brands. This is an alloy consisting of one-half gold and one-half silver (twenty-four karats is pure gold). The better brands are quite silvery in color with only a very slight yellowish tinge, and are used by many sign painters in place of silver leaf. Its workability is midway between gold and silver. White gold is practical to use for single-gild applications over varnish centers, although some slight tarnishing is to be expected in time.

**Silver Leaf**    This is used only for burnished glass work, as it tarnishes rapidly in contact with paint and varnish or when exposed to air. The cost is about one-third that of gold leaf. Silver leaf is about three times as thick as gold leaf and consequently is more difficult to apply. There is considerable difference in thickness between different brands of silver leaf; the domestic brands are ordinarily much thinner than imported varieties and are much easier to work with.

**Palladium Leaf**    This is a silvery metal of the platinum family. It costs a little more than gold leaf. It is used in place of silver for applications where the tarnishing of silver could not be tolerated, such as single-gild, matte-center work on glass.

Palladium is darker than silver and has a slight brownish color. Being thinner than silver leaf, it is easier to handle for burnished gilding, but removing the excess after backing up is very difficult. The general use of palladium leaf in place of silver is not recommended; a better choice is 12-karat white gold. Palladium is not as available as in the past, since sign painters now substitute white gold.

**Aluminum Leaf**

Aluminum leaf is too thick for burnished gilding on glass, but is widely used for surface gilding. It can be rubbed with a little more pressure than can gold and calls for a much stronger tack (wetter size). Aluminum leaf should be applied just as soon as the size can be touched lightly with a dry knuckle without coming away on the skin, instead of when the size has reached the whistle tack needed for gold. Size for aluminum leaf is customarily colored with white instead of yellow, because yellow shows through cracks in the leaf, which are difficult to totally avoid and have a tendency to become visible through pinholes after a time. Cracks and pinholes can be further disguised by dusting aluminum powder over the surface after gilding.

Aluminum leaf is useful for matte portions of silver lettering in combination with burnished silver or white gold, as it will not tarnish. Its cost per book (5 1/2 inches square) is far less than that of gold leaf. It also varies greatly in thickness; for matte centers in glass work and for general surface gilding, the thinner varieties are preferable. Although some European brands have a high luster, they may be almost as thick as foil; they are useful for backing up window lettering as extra protection under severe service and for backing pearl, both to make it shine and to protect it.

**Variegated Leaf**

This is a copper alloy leaf which is given an oxidizing treatment in manufacture, resulting in a patchwork of different colorations that usually range from reddish to green, blue, and purple. It is used on glass work for matte centers in combination with burnished gold outlines, especially for signs needing a splash of color (for example, those with an oriental character) and for accents and letter styles with flashy characteristics in varnished surface work.

# 2 Glass Gilding

Nothing conveys as much impact on a window as gold leaf. Gold leaf has dignity and richness and, in addition, provides something that no other material can: *movement*. Being highly reflective, it changes subtly as a person passes by or as it catches the movement of traffic. As a result, gold catches the eye as no other material does.

There is nothing as soul-satisfying to a sign painter as the ability to do a creditable job of glass gilding. To be sure, this involves learning some tricky techniques. The many treatments possible in glass gilding require considerable skill and a thorough knowledge of materials. Those who succeed in mastering every phase of this work can properly be called the aristocracy of the sign trade. Good glass men are not plentiful anymore, and few of them are ever out of work. This is something to which to aspire.

However, the simpler types of glass gilding are not so difficult to learn as to be beyond the ability of anyone who has learned basic brush lettering and can execute a good quality of workmanship with ease. When such a novice sign painter has absorbed the description of the basic process, he should be able to turn out an acceptable job of burnished gilding on the first attempt. Mastery of the more involved techniques will follow with perseverance. If at all possible, one should also attend seminars or national meetings at which demonstrations of how to actually proceed with a job are given.

Traveling around the country, one may notice an appalling lack of variety in glass gilding. With a few noticeable exceptions, most large cities exhibit one characteristic style of window lettering that is done over and over, so that a visitor would suppose that all the work was done by the same person, and one with very little imagination at that. Glass gilding allows infinite variety of treatment. It is possible to vary layout, letter styles, and combinations of colors and burnished and matte finishes. Sign painters should make all these techniques work for them. It is an unhappy truth that fine letter proportions and clean workmanship do not impress the public as much as they should, but a customer is quick to notice and is appreciative when you succeed in giving him something a little different. Often that little extra can be provided at no extra charge to the customer, but adds to both his and your satisfaction in the work, providing a base for selling other topnotch jobs. Don't be satisfied to learn just one style of glass gilding and confine yourself to that. As soon as you have learned to do a simple job with matte

5

centers, you will already have nine-tenths of the know-how necessary to do all the rest. A look through old textbooks and magazines, as well as portfolios of other craftsmen, will give you infinite ideas of ways to proceed.

## The Basic Process: Burnished Gilding with Gelatin Water Size

Very briefly, the steps in laying gold leaf are as follows. The inscription is laid out on the outside of the glass, either with grease pencil or with a pounce pattern. The glass on the inside, where the work will be done, is then cleaned very thoroughly. Leaf is adhered to the glass with water size made by dissolving gelatin in hot water. The water size is flowed onto the glass with a soft brush known as a *water-size brush*. Pieces of leaf are applied to the wet glass with a special brush, the *gilding tip*, in sufficient number to overlap a trifle in order to cover the inscription completely.

When the leaf has dried, it is burnished or polished down lightly with absorbent cotton. Then a second application of water size is flowed over the leaf in order to bring it to a high luster. At this stage, while flowing the water size over the first gild, any holes or holidays are patched by applying small pieces of leaf over them. This operation is known as the *second gild*.

When the second gild is dry, it, too, is burnished with cotton, using a little more pressure and being careful so as not to scratch or mar the gild. The lettering or design is then painted on the back of the leaf, in reverse, with quick-drying paint. This is called *backing up*.

When the backing paint is dry, excess leaf outside of the painted portions is removed with damp cotton. This is possible because the gelatin that adheres the gold is water-soluble and can be dissolved in all those portions that have not been painted over. The painted areas remain to form the inscription in burnished gold as seen from the outside of the window. An outline or a shade can be added at this stage, or the inscription can be left plain.

Finally, a protective coat of varnish is applied with a lettering brush over the back of the inscription, so that it will withstand being washed.

Each of these operations is described in detail in the pages that follow. Your attention is directed to the index and the troubleshooting checklist on page 153.

## Gilding Tools

Gelatin water size is flowed onto the glass with a short, thick, camel-hair brush, shown in Figure 1. These brushes are made in various widths, a convenient width being two inches. Select a water-size brush as thick as possible, preferably one that will carry a good charge of water size. Avoid steel-bound brushes that will rust and cause much trouble. Don't limit yourself on price. A good size brush is a pleasure to work with and will last a long time, thirty years or more if well cared for. (The brush shown in Figure 1 had been in use for 25 years and was still in fine shape when the photograph was taken.)

The water-size brush must be kept scrupulously clean, preferably stored in a special compartment reserved for it in the kit where it will be protected from oil spatters and dust. If this is not feasible, keep the brush wrapped in aluminum foil or in a plastic bag when not in use. Never allow the size brush to come in contact with anything oily or greasy. Rinse it thoroughly after every use, preferably with warm water.

The gilding tip consists of a thin layer of camel or badger hair bound between two pieces of stiff cardboard. The camel-hair tips are for handling gold leaf; the badger tips are for silver and other heavier leaves.

**Figure 1.** Two gilding tips (left and right) and a water-size brush.

However, it is possible to use only the camel-hair tip for all kinds of leaf. Tips are made in single and double thicknesses and in a variety of lengths to suit individual tastes. A long (2 3/4 in.), single-thick gilding tip is one size that many find easiest to use in placing leaf with precision.

Gilding tips are made about 3 1/2 inches wide. Some glass gilders find this to be wider than necessary and clumsy to handle, so they cut away the hair about 3/4 in. from each edge, like the tip shown at right in Figure 1. Such a cut-down tip will minimize the possibility of touching the wet glass with the hair, yet will pick up leaf just as well as a full-size tip.

A somewhat thinner tip is also easier for many sign painters to charge for picking up leaf, and some will use one that is quite thin. To thin-out a tip to individual taste, run a razor blade along the base of the hair, cutting a single row of hairs at a time until the desired thickness is met. Observation of the illustrations in this book should give one the idea of a good, workable thickness.

The gilding tip must also be kept clean and flat. When not in use, it is advisable to keep it wrapped in paper or between two pieces of cardboard. The tip can be washed in cold water and mild soap once in a while to clean off caked rouge, after which it should be combed carefully and hung to dry. This will restore straightness to the hair. Combing the tip on the job to clear it of small pieces of leaf and rouge will prolong its life and good working characteristics.

## Grease-Pencil Layouts

For small, uncomplicated gold leaf jobs, it is often convenient to lay out the inscription with grease pencil on the outside of the glass, rather than make an extra trip to measure windows for patterns. (See Figure 2.) Gold leaf is transparent enough so that the marks can be seen through the leaf from the inside of the window. This method doesn't work with silver or other opaque leaves. It can be managed, however, by penciling the letter spacing above the line, where it can be seen over the top of the leaf as shown in Figure 2-b. The darker grease pencils, china markers or *Stabilo* pencils are excellent

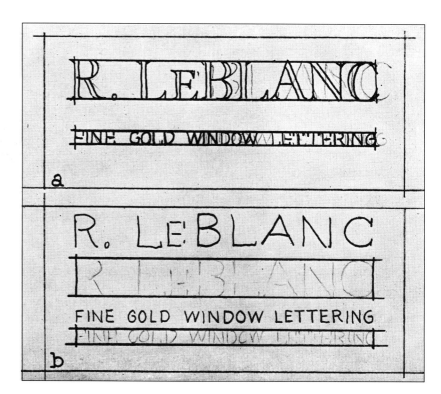

**Figure 2.** Grease pencil layouts: (a) for normal gold leaf gilding; (b) for gilding with silver or other opaque leaves.

for this purpose. Lighter colors are better for tinted glass; some sign painters prefer red or even use chalk.

When laying out with a grease pencil, make heavy top and bottom lines, work out the letter spacing with very light strokes until the spacing is adjusted properly, then go over the spacing lines with heavy strokes. It is very confusing to try to follow a jumble of lines when viewing them through a layer of leaf.

At times it may be difficult to see grease pencil lines through the leaf because of dark objects in the background, such as parked cars or shrubbery, or because of dark buildings across the street. In such cases it helps to tack a sheet of tracing paper or even ordinary sign paper over the layout on the outside of the glass.

Needless to say, when working from a grease pencil layout, you must try to avoid excessive patching of the gild, for it is difficult to see pencil marks through two layers of leaf.

**Pounce Patterns**

These are made by drawing the inscription on paper with as much detail as may be required, then perforating the lines with a pounce wheel, as shown in Figure 3. To transfer to the glass or other surface, the pattern is placed in position and held with masking tape, then dusted with a pounce bag containing either light or dark powder, depending on which will show better under existing conditions. The powder will go through the perforations and leave the design outlined on the working surface.

It is possible to prepare a much more accurate layout with this technique than can be done by marking directly on the glass with grease pencil or chalk, and so it is best to use a pounce pattern whenever the

**Figure 3.** Use of a pounce wheel to perforate a pattern for glass gilding.

inscription is at all intricate. For glass gilding, the pattern is applied first on the outside of the glass as a guide for laying the leaf, then applied again on the inside directly on top of the leaf, as a guide for backing up. The gild can be backed up much faster and with greater assurance with the layout directly on the leaf, making up for much of the "extra" time spent in making the pattern.

There are several other advantages to using pounce patterns. If the inscription is to be done more than once, the advantage is obvious. Patterns are saved in case a window should be broken or if, for any reason, the inscription has to be done again at a later date. In addition, the use of a pounce pattern makes it easy to alter the layout by shifting the pattern when pouncing different areas. You will often want to make such minor changes in a layout when it is examined actually on the window.

When making patterns for glass work, use a fine pounce wheel, one that makes holes that are small without being so fine that they cause the pattern to tear easily. A heavy deposit of powder from a large wheel is troublesome on glass work because of the tendency of backing paint to mix with the pounce powder and cause weak or ragged edges.

Perforating is done on top of a soft material such as Homasote board, but heavy felt, cork, soft rubber, foam board and Celotex board are also good. Cardboard or paper composition board are sometimes used, but because these are hard they will dull your wheel and do not allow a clean hole in the paper. An electric perforator will eliminate these problems.

When using a wheel, turn the pattern over after it has been completely pounced and sandpaper the perforations lightly to open them up so the pounce powder will pass easily through them (Figure 4). This step can be eliminated when using an electric perforator. Next dust the paper well to remove the paper fiber dust, which can be even more troublesome than the pounce powder during the backing-up operation. An ostrich-feather duster is handy for this, as it will pick up all leftover fibers and other dust from the pattern that might contaminate the paint.

**Figure 4.** Sanding the back of the pattern to open up the perforations.

Since a heavy deposit of powder is likely to interfere with the backing paint, pounce bags for glass work should not permit the powder to pass through too freely. Use tightly woven broadcloth, heavy men's stocking material, an empty Bull Durham pouch, hardware parts bag, or some similar material. Pounce bags are made by placing a suitable quantity of powder in the middle of a square of cloth, then topping it with a sizeable wad of cotton. The cotton provides inexpensive bulk and a soft center for continuous pouncing on a soft surface such as gold. If the bag is filled entirely with powder, the cloth is certain to wear out before the powder is all used up. The ends of the cloth are gathered in a bunch at the back and secured with masking tape or string. Suitable and reasonably priced, ready-made pounce bags are available with black, blue, or white powder from sign supply houses.

The inscription is pounced on the outside of the window by gently tapping the pounce bag here and there along the pattern to deposit powder on the paper. Then use the bag to rub over every part of the inscription. (See Figures 5 and 6.)

When working from a pounce pattern, remember to make registration marks at the time the pattern is applied on the outside of the window so that the pattern can be placed in the same position on the inside when it is time to back up. A simple way to do this is to dab the pounce bag across the two top corners of the paper. (See Figure 6.) But if the job isn't to be completed on the same day, if there is heavy traffic at the door, or if bad weather threatens, it is safer to make registration marks across top, sides and bottom with grease pencil.

Care must be taken when repositioning the pattern on the inside when working on thick or double thermal-pane glass. The thickness of the glass can throw your pattern off by as much as an inch in some cases. Each registration position should be viewed from as close to the same position as possible to avoid this problem.

More information and suggestions for making pounce patterns will be found in Chapter 10.

**Figure 5.** Pouncing the pattern on the outside of the glass preparatory to gilding.

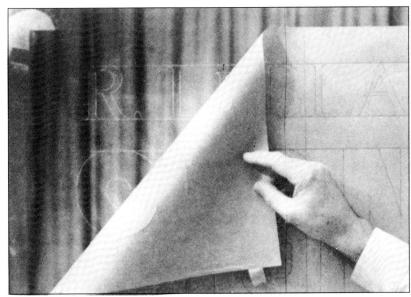

**Figure 6.** The inscription transferred to the glass. Note the registration mark made by dabbing the pounce bag over the corner of the paper.

## Placement on Window

One of the saddest experiences in sign work is completing a well-executed leaf inscription on a window, then going across the street to admire the fruits of your labor and having to admit that it should have been a little higher, or that it isn't quite straight, or that it isn't in the best position.

In general, large inscriptions that run across most of the window should be placed high enough so that they can be read from across the street over the tops of parked cars. The proper position for small corner inscriptions is one or two feet below eye level, depending somewhat on the height of the window floor. In some cases, a peculiarity of the window display may make a different position advisable, and this point should be checked with the customer.

In checking the layout for straightness, measuring from both ends of the lettering to the bottom of the window is usually sufficient, but you should first check to see that the bottom of the window is level. Often the settling of an old building will have dragged the windows out of line, particularly in stores that have central doorways. In such cases it is better to place the lettering in a level position. Don't trust your eye; use a carpenter's level. Some situations will require placement that is not level, but complements an unusual frame or other trim.

It is bad layout practice to allow lettering to crowd the edges of a window; make the letters a little smaller to keep them a foot or more away from the edges. Corner inscriptions also should not be placed too near the edges of the glass. Keep them 6 in. to 10 in. away from the corner; they will look better and you won't be cramped while working on them from the inside of the window.

In this connection it is worth mentioning that customers will frequently specify a letter size that is much too large for the window. It is part of our job to point this out and to advise the customer as to the proper size of lettering that will make a dignified-looking sign. Gold lettering will claim sufficient attention without shouting.

## Cleaning the Glass

For successful water-size gilding, the surface of the glass on which gilding is to be done must be cleaned very thoroughly. No halfway measures will do. Ordinary cake Bon Ami provides satisfactory cleaning on most windows. With a wad of wet cotton or sponge, rub up a generous amount from the cake and give the glass a good scrubbing (Figure 7). Allow the Bon Ami lather to dry, then wipe off the powder with a clean cotton or a soft clean rag. Then clean again, using new cotton or rag, for any oily or greasy film that may have been picked up on the rag during the first cleaning may transfer back to the glass on the second cleaning. If your area's water is hard or heavily chlorinated, it might be wise to use distilled water for cleanup to avoid possible contaminates in the water, as well.

Windows will sometimes have films that are especially difficult to remove. Among these are films from tobacco smoke and cleaning compounds that contain wax, especially aerosol window cleaners. Bon Ami has a built-in indicator for trouble of this sort, which is that in such cases you will find the dry powder difficult to wipe off. When this occurs, repeat the cleaning operation with Bon Ami until the glass wipes clean easily.

The popularity of window cleaning compounds containing wax or silicone creates problems for the sign painter. Silicone compounds in particular are very troublesome. They will cause crawling in the water size and general poor adhesion of paint or varnish, and they are very difficult to remove from the glass. Repeated scrubbing with Bon Ami will usually clean them off. You might also try cleaning the glass first with DuPont's *Prep-Sol*, which is a silicone solvent obtainable from automotive paint dealers. One of the major glass companies also recommends cleaning glass with a paste made by mixing whiting or 4F pumice and isopropyl alcohol (non-perfumed rubbing alcohol or *Ever-Clear*). A non-sudsing ammonia can also be used with whiting or Bon Ami.

Paint adhesion on newly installed plate glass is a special problem and is not necessarily connected with cleaning the surface. It is a puzzling

fact that the gild is more likely to peel after a short period of service if the glass was new at the time the job was done. New glass does not have a coating of some oily or waxy substance, as one would suppose. Major glass companies assure their customers that new glass leaves the factory with the surfaces absolutely clean. It is possible that paint clings better to old glass simply because the surface has become pitted and scratched to some extent by repeated washings. However, another source of information indicates that new glass has a difference in molecular structure that might account for poor adhesion of lettering.

This is explained in terms of free sodium and calcium ions, which tend to migrate to the surfaces. These may be numerous on new glass, but are gradually removed by repeated washing. We know that sodium and calcium are alkali metals, that alkalis readily combine with oil (from the paint) to form soaps, and that soap is well-known as an anti-sticking agent. So it doesn't seem too farfetched to suppose that some peeling in the paint might derive from this source. A special cleaning material for cleaning new glass, possibly something similar to the tin chloride that mirror makers use to cause the silver to adhere, might be effective. Prep-Sol, mentioned earlier, seems to ease this problem and certainly cleans tinted and architectural glass better than Bon Ami.

The importance of cleaning glass thoroughly before gilding cannot be stressed too much. Do a good job of cleaning the glass and you will spare yourself many, many headaches in the subsequent operations.

## Making Water Size

Water size is made by dissolving gelatin capsules in warm water. The directions usually found in sign literature call for boiling water and this is the way apprentices were taught to make it "in the old days."

Gelatin is a highly complex substance and one that undergoes changes readily. It has a cellular structure that permits it to absorb water like a sponge. When saturated with water, it becomes soft and jellylike, but when the water evaporates it reverts to the solid stage and becomes much tougher than it was originally. (A chamois skin exhibits the same property, as you may know.) Although weak solutions remain liquid upon cooling, they also revert to jelly and eventually to a tough, solid stage as the water gradually evaporates. Gelatin dissolves completely in hot water but can be dissolved much more easily if it is soaked in cold water beforehand.

In the following directions for making water size, you will see how this information can be useful. These directions have been evolved as a result of much experimentation over a period of years and, if followed carefully, will help you avoid many causes of aggravation in your gilding.

Obtain a supply of No. 00 empty gelatin capsules. These are the kind used for medicine and can be purchased through pharmacies or most sign supply houses that carry gilders' supplies. Store them in a closed glass jar or a metal box, because if the gelatin is allowed to absorb moisture freely from the air, it will in time become hardened and difficult to dissolve.

Any clean aluminum, stainless steel or enameled vessel of convenient shape and capacity can be used for a size pail. Even a stainless steel can that started out in life as a photographic film developing tank works well and holds about one and one-half pints. The space available in your kit will, of course, determine the dimensions best suited for your use. A small aluminum can that holds one-half pint is handy for small jobs and takes up little room in the kit. Like all other gilding tools, it must be kept clean and protected against all contact with oil or grease. The size pail should be rinsed thoroughly after each use, preferably with warm water, and it is a good plan to give it a thorough scrubbing with scouring powder once in a while, perhaps after every four or five jobs.

Gelatin capsules made by different manufacturers vary somewhat in thickness. The following proportions may need to be adjusted slightly, but, being somewhat on the high side, will constitute a safe guide. For adhering all types of gold leaf and the thinner brands of silver leaf, use two 00 capsules per pint of size. Heavier brands of silver leaf will require a stronger size: use two and one-half to three capsules per pint of size. Palladium leaf, a tough metal that is difficult to clean off the glass, requires a weak size; use one or one and one-half 00 capsules per pint of size.

Drop the required number of *opened* capsules (that is, with the two halves separated) into your size pail. Add enough cold water to just cover the capsules. If your local water supply has a high mineral content (hard water) or contains other impurities that may cause cloudiness in the gild, using distilled water may be advisable. Be sure to use only distilled water, as natural, purified or artesian water is not void of impurities that might harm the gild. Never use water that has a sulfur content when gilding with silver, as it will tarnish the leaf.

Make sure that the capsules are filled with water by holding them under water and squeezing the air out of them with the fingers. Allow the capsules to soak in the cold water for ten to fifteen minutes or longer, which will cause them to swell to about twice their normal size and dissolve very easily. Heat the contents of the pail gently and only long enough to dissolve the gelatin completely. *Don't boil the size.* Boiling is unnecessary when the gelatin has been soaked in cold water and only makes it more difficult to clean off the excess leaf afterward. Keep the size pail in motion all the time during the heating operation to prevent the capsules from sticking

**Figure 8.** Heating the water size.

to the bottom or sides of the pail. If they do stick, they will become almost impossible to dissolve completely, and, of course, if the gelatin isn't all dissolved, the size will be too weak.

*Sterno Canned Heat* provides a convenient means for heating size. This may be bought at most drug and hardware stores and at some sporting goods stores. A small can is convenient to carry in the kit and will be sufficient for several jobs. Sterno provides a very hot flame with a maximum of safety, since it cannot spill and is not explosive by nature. No special stove is necessary; just hold the size pail in the fingers near the top and keep it about an inch above the Sterno can, as in Figure 8. This makes it easy to keep the pail in motion while heating the mixture. When the gelatin has been dissolved, the Sterno flame is extinguished simply by lowering the size pail onto the top of the Sterno can. Caution: Don't try to pick up the Sterno can immediately. You will discover that it is quite hot. The bottom of the can stays relatively cool, however, and seldom damages any surface underneath. It is still a good idea to set the can on top of your kit so that the customer's table top or window sill is not damaged.

Now you can add enough cold water to make up the required amount of size, and it is ready for use. There is no point in heating the size. It is used cold. Also, it shouldn't be necessary to strain the size before use if the gelatin is completely dissolved and if the size pail and water supply are clean.

Gelatin size must be made on the same day that it is to be used. Since it is an animal product, it may spoil and thus lose much of its adhesive ability after standing overnight. Under certain climatic conditions, size can

15

go stale during the day and might need to be made again midway through the day, after lunch, for instance. Heavier mixtures may spoil more rapidly than thinner ones.

Size can be made up in the shop before going to the job, or it can be prepared on the job. The latter choice means less weight to carry to the job and also avoids the chance of getting the inside of the sign kit all wet from spilling. It also does no harm for the customer to get to see all the operations involved in doing his job. If you elect to make up size on the job, you can save time by following this sequence of operations: upon arrival, start the capsules soaking; while they are soaking you can proceed to lay out the job and clean the glass; by the time the glass is ready, the capsules should be well softened and ready to be heated. It does no harm if the capsules soak longer than necessary.

## Gilding

Following is one sign painter's personal method of handling leaf described in considerable detail for the benefit of the novice. Every experienced gilder has his own peculiar methods, and none is necessarily better for everyone; however, if the beginner will carefully follow the directions given here, down to the smallest detail, he will be spared the more common gilding difficulties. As he becomes proficient, he will no doubt find little departures that will be more comfortable for him.

First study the layout and decide how large the pieces of leaf should be cut so as to cover the inscription most efficiently. The rule is to use the largest pieces possible; don't try to cut the leaf to fit the letter strokes exactly in an attempt to save gold. You will take more time to do the job and you may find that you are using more rather than less gold, as there is some loss during cutting. Also your time is more valuable than a few extra leaves used in gilding large pieces.

Leaf must be applied so as to cover the letters completely and overlap a trifle. Lines of lettering up to about 4 in. in height are best gilded solid, using big pieces of leaf. Larger letters can be gilded by laying pieces of leaf along the letter strokes. The width of the letter stroke will then determine the best way to cut the leaf. Even when gold is to be used only for outlines, the letters are usually gilded solid unless they are very large, since it makes more sense to apply one big piece of leaf rather than two smaller pieces that, together, represent just as much gold. Figure 9 shows examples of various types of placement of leaf for different sizes of lettering.

The easiest piece of leaf to handle is the half leaf, and beginners may want to confine themselves to pieces of this size at first. As your skill increases, you can progress to handling thirds, combinations of thirds and two-thirds for large letters, fourths for thin lines, and finally the whole leaf, which represents the acme of skill.

Gilding can be done either from left to right or from right to left. A case can be made out for either method. For right-handed gilders, it is a little easier to place the leaf with precision starting from the left as the work already done will not be obscured by your hand and the tip when you place additional leaf; also, it is a little easier to obtain a smooth gild when working this way. However, working from right to left has the advantage that you are less likely to touch the wet glass with the hair of the tip. If the hair of the tip touches the sized area where you have not yet placed leaf, it will

**Figure 9.** Various methods of cutting and placing leaf for different sizes of lettering. The top line is gilded with full leaves, the bottom line with half leaves placed horizontally. In the word "Signs," which will be backed up in outline only, the first three letters have been gilded by cutting the leaf into alternate thirds and two-thirds pieces; the last two letters are gilded entirely with fourths. The first letter S, gilded with big pieces, took four leaves, whereas the last S, gilded with smaller pieces, required only three leaves. However, this letter took twice as long to gild. It will be seen that the first three letters of the word "Signs" could have been gilded solid by cutting the leaf in this fashion.

make the size crawl away from the point of contact and prevent the leaf from straightening itself out on the glass. This will also leave holes in the gild. The illustrations in the book are gilded from right to left for this reason, but you should try it both ways. Depending on the various job conditions, either method may be better than the other.

Pieces of leaf can be placed on the glass either horizontally or vertically. Horizontal pieces can be applied from either above or below the line. It is a little easier to get the leaf on smoothly by applying from above as the leaf then hangs down from the tip in a flat position. But when you acquire skill, you will find that applying the leaf from below is faster and less tiring–you don't have to reach so far.

Whichever position is used, you must pick up the leaf so that one end overhangs the gilding tip. Place the end of the piece of leaf toward the open area of the glass, so that no hair from the tip will touch the glass where you have not yet applied leaf (Figure 10). Similarly, when leaf is applied vertically on large letters, the leaf must overhang the tip at the bottom, where other pieces of leaf are to be placed.

Begin the actual gilding procedure by dipping the water-size brush into the pail of size and moving it around until it becomes saturated. Carry it dripping wet to the glass, and flow on a good layer of size over the first portion of the inscription. This step–getting plenty of water on the glass–is the secret for getting a smooth gild. When there is a good layer of size between the leaf and the glass, each piece of leaf will float on the surface of the size as it is placed in position, and if the leaf goes on a bit wrinkled it will straighten itself out with a little pop. But if the layer of size is thin, the leaf will stay just as it leaves the tip, wrinkles and all.

Apply size to cover an area just large enough for a few pieces of leaf, as many as you can lay before the size starts to thin out and dry. Of course, if you find that you have sized too big an area, you can always go over part of it again with more size, but this isn't good practice; the additional layer of gelatin under the leaf tends to cloud the gild and makes it more

17

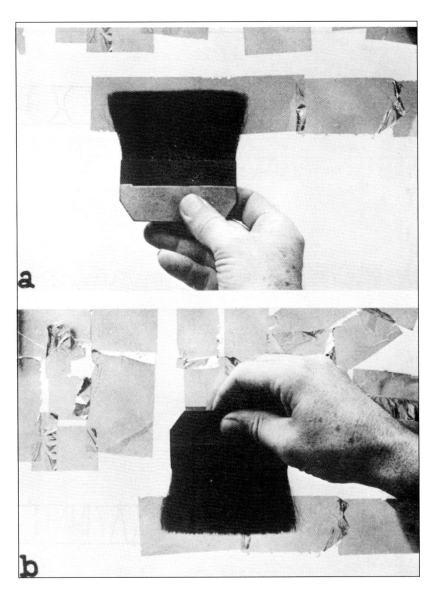

**Figure 10.** Two methods of placing horizontal pieces of leaf: (a) from below and (b) from above the line. Note that the leaf overhangs the tip on the left in either case, so that hair from the tip won't touch the wet glass.

difficult to clean off the excess leaf afterward. The best method is to keep the area wet by adding more size to it as you gild so that the size doesn't actually dry. On the second gild, or when touching up, be more careful to size a smaller area.

If you have never handled gold leaf before, follow these directions for getting a piece of leaf out of the book and onto the glass, whether you are right- or left-handed. Holding the book in a horizontal position in the left hand, fold the cover page neatly underneath. Develop the habit of folding back the book pages neatly and without wrinkles. If you do this carelessly, you will find that the entire operation becomes clumsy and you will spoil a lot of leaf. Still holding the book in the left hand, grasp the gilding tip under the book between the middle and fourth fingers, hair toward the open end. The handle serves as a support for the book while you fold the rouged paper and cut the leaf. Many prefer to use a piece of cardboard under the book for

this purpose, but this gives you another item to shuffle and poses the problem of what to do with the tip while manipulating the book.

Fan out the book pages slightly with a little twisting pressure of the thumb so that you can catch the pages at the side one at a time. Next, very carefully lift one corner of the first rouged sheet, which will expose the first leaf of gold (Figure 11). As you lift the rouged paper, make sure that the gold intends to lie flat and doesn't want to come up with the paper that you are turning back. This will often happen, especially in cold, dry weather, due to static in the book. When you encounter this, let the rouged paper down again and breathe heavily on top of it. The moisture in your breath will discharge the static and permit the paper to come free from the gold.

We will assume that you are going to gild with half-leaves. Turn the rouged paper halfway back and crease it down the middle horizontally, leaving half of the leaf of gold exposed (Figure 12). If the gold wrinkles or folds during this operation, blow gently on it to flatten it out nicely. With practice, wrinkles or folds will not happen often. Now cut the gold by drawing a fingernail across it using the edge of the fold in the turned-back paper as a guide (Figure 13). Very little pressure is needed. This operation must be done as shown by reaching across the back of the book, so that the fingertip slides on top of the paper and not on the gold. Don't try it the other way around; you will roll up the gold into a nice little ball. If the leaf still rolls or tears under your fingernail, it may be because the nail is rough; polish it by rubbing it briskly on a trouser leg. A moist fingertip may also cause trouble.

Some brands of gold leaf are more difficult to cut than others, and silver leaf is always more difficult to cut than gold. If you have difficulty in cutting the leaf, try rubbing up a little rouge on the fingernail by scratching the rouged paper. This often helps.

When the leaf has been cut, transfer the gilding tip to your right hand and draw it across the hair of your head, softly and slowly two or three times to charge it with oil (Figure 14). Don't overdo this or you might find it difficult to get the leaf to come away from the tip and onto the glass. Most

**Figure 12.** Folding the rouged paper, leaving half the leaf of gold exposed.

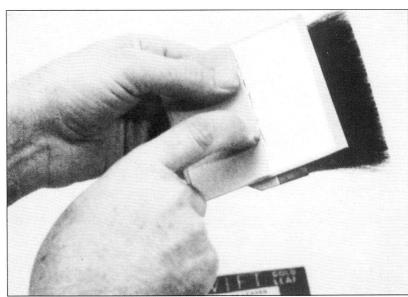

**Figure 13.** Cutting the leaf with the fingernail, using the folded edge of the paper as a guide. Note how the cardboard and back of the tip serve as supports for the book while making the cut.

people suppose that this is done to pick up electricity. Actually it is done to charge the tip with oil, which gives the tip just the right amount of stickiness to enable it to pick up leaf. This also explains why water size will crawl away from any spot touched by the tip. New tips will have to be used for a while before they will pick up oil easily enough to work well. Likewise, as mentioned before, it is important to wash the tip regularly to keep down oil and rouge build-up, which can cause obvious problems.

Some gilders may be inclined to disagree with this oil theory. It is true that stroking the tip through the hair can also generate static, especially if it is done briskly. A static charge on the tip will enable it to pick up leaf, but is a nuisance in glass gilding, because the static transfers to the book pages and causes the leaf to stick. Moreover, static in the tip causes the gold to

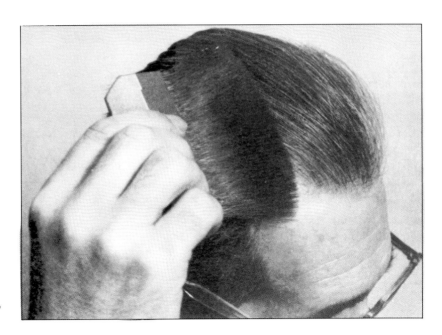

**Figure 14.** Charging the tip with oil from the hair.

jump from the book to the tip and so encourages wrinkling. The higher the oil content of your hair, the less static will be generated and the more readily the tip will pick up leaf.

Don't stroke the tip through the hair too much or too often, especially when working with gold leaf, or you might find it difficult to get the leaf to come away from the tip and onto the glass. About two strokes through the hair after every four or five pieces of leaf is plenty, depending on atmospheric conditions. You will begin to develop a feel for when to charge the tip again as you work. Laying silver leaf requires a much stronger charge than does gold, and you may find it difficult to pick up enough oil on a camel-hair tip, especially if your hair is dry. Badger tips are made for handling silver leaf. They are stiffer than camel hair and so tend to pick up oil more readily. (Since white gold is so often used in place of silver, many will not need to invest in a badger tip; however, some special effects seem to call for the use of silver.) Although either tip can be used successfully, a good badger tip can make for speedier handling of silver even though the stiffer hair takes some degree of practice to work easily. When it is difficult to pick up leaf with your tips, one remedy for the situation may be to rub a little Vaseline or Vaseline hair tonic into your hair, an operation which is often misunderstood by the sidewalk audience, but which gets the job done effectively.

The better areas to charge the tip, depending on the condition of your hair, are usually behind the ears, along the sideburns, across the forehead, or along the edge of a beard. Ladies find the forehead at the hair line most effective. Your forearm may also be used, although additional Vaseline there may help. Incidentally, sign painters are often asked, "What would you do if you were bald?" This is such a frequent query heard by sign painters that a sign concern once had one of their employees, a baldheaded man, work as a gag in the window of the shop with a black cat, which he used for charging his tip. Some baldheaded men, though, have found that stroking the tip on the

21

**Figure 15.** Picking up the leaf with the tip. The tip is placed on the leaf about halfway. Note that the leaf is allowed to overhang the tip at one end.

scalp works just fine. So don't bother taking out baldness insurance. Once the gilding tip is charged, place the hair of the tip on the piece of leaf that you have cut, about half on and half off, with the leaf extending beyond the tip at one end, as previously explained. Give the tip a little twist or a little jerk to tear the cut leaf away from the book (Figure 15) and lift it off the book at the open end.

Bring the piece of leaf toward the glass, meanwhile concentrating on the exact position where it is to go. When you get it within half an inch or so of the glass, speed up the movement of the tip, so that the leaf is placed onto the glass with a little slapping motion (Figure 16).

Don't hesitate at this point, for as soon as any portion of the leaf touches the wet glass, capillary action goes to work and pulls the leaf quickly and strongly. If the leaf is being held back by the tip at the same time, it is likely to be badly wrinkled or torn. Once the piece of leaf has left the book, the motion of the tip should be continuous until the leaf is on the glass. By keeping the tip in constant motion, the pressure of the air against the leaf keeps it flat and tight against the tip. If the forward motion stops, the leaf has a chance to droop and wrinkle. If your delivery is correct, the leaf should go onto the glass smoothly, and, even if there is a trace of wrinkling, it will usually smooth itself out as the leaf floats on the wet size.

The first piece of leaf applied may want to slide down, since the size has just been applied and may still be flowing, so keep your eye on it a moment; if it starts to slide, push it back with a corner of the tip, applied to the center of the leaf. You can check its further descent by pressing hard with a fingertip on the top edge of the leaf, holding the finger there during a slow count to ten (Figure 17).

If all this seems terribly complicated at this time, and your first attempt to follow the instructions is laborious and not entirely successful, don't be discouraged; by the time you have laid a hundred pieces or so, they will be going on much faster and more smoothly. Read and re-read this section a few times both before and as you practice to help avoid difficulty.

Now for the second piece of leaf. Fold the paper page all the way back and neatly under the book. Place the tip on the second leaf now exposed. Give the tip a little twist, as before, and off comes the leaf. You may find it easier to turn the book around and lift the second piece off the back: Try

Figure 16. Carrying the leaf to the glass.

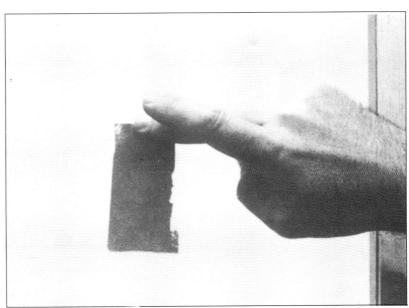

Figure 17. Stopping the leaf from sliding by pressing against the top edge with a fingertip. The second finger is used so that the index finger will be dry for cutting the next piece of leaf.

it both ways. After you have learned this step well, turning the book may become cumbersome, slowing your progress. Lay the piece of leaf onto the glass in the same manner as the first piece, overlapping the second piece by a quarter of an inch or so. If the first piece has stopped sliding, it will hold the second piece in place also.

When you have become proficient in handling half-leaves of gold, you can try cutting the leaf into thirds (Figure 18). These are not difficult to handle, although a more delicate touch is needed while cutting and lifting the narrower pieces out of the book, for they tear easily. A little difficulty may be experienced in getting the middle section of a leaf out of the book,

**Figure 18.** Cutting leaf into thirds.

for this piece will have two cut edges to hold it to the paper. Remember to give the tip a little twist to free the leaf before trying to lift it off the book.

For gilding long, thin lines, you can cut the leaf into fourths. These are the narrowest pieces that are practical to work with. They must be cut skillfully, for they tear very easily. You must also remember to keep the pressure of your nail just heavy enough to cut without marring the leaf underneath, as the mark from cutting will not burnish out and will show as a light line in the finished letter. This is especially true of books made of very thin paper. The books with heavier paper, usually containing domestic gold, are therefore worth some consideration even though they are more expensive than others.

When a half-leaf is not quite wide enough to cover the letter stroke of a large letter, the page may be cut into thirds and two-thirds. First cut and lay a two-thirds piece, then add two one-third pieces side by side, and repeat.

Now we can consider handling of the full leaf. In order to gild successfully with full leaves, conditions must be close to ideal. The air in the vicinity of the work must be still, and it will be especially important to maintain a good flow of size on the glass. The leaf is picked up with about a third of its width on the tip, as shown in Figure 16 (but with the tip at the side instead of at the top), then carried to the glass and laid in place in one sweeping motion so that the free end of the leaf is thrown forward as the tip reaches the glass. Your aim with the leaf has to be especially good, as you cannot stop the motion of the tip toward the glass in order to place the leaf exactly. It's a little tricky, but anyone can learn to do it after developing skill in handling smaller pieces. Handling the full leaf requires confidence more than anything else. These big pieces save a lot of time when there are large areas to cover, and their use eliminates patching a lot of overlaps.

Continue to lay pieces of leaf until you have come almost to the edge of the sized area, leaving a strip of wet glass to be overlapped with the next application of size. If size is applied over the leaf before it has dried completely, the wet leaf will be wiped right off; instead, size another section and continue gilding. Be sure to apply leaf first on the remainder of the preceding sized section, as that will be the first to dry. Continue gilding in sections in this fashion until the entire inscription is covered with leaf.

When an inscription contains more than one line of lettering, the water size applied to the top line will run in streaks down the glass and across the area to be occupied by the bottom lines. If the streaks dry on the glass and are gilded over, they will show as yellow lines in the finished gild. Moreover, removing excess leaf will be difficult in these areas. On small inscriptions, this can be overcome by keeping the entire inscription flooded with size while the top lines are being gilded. On larger jobs it is simpler to disregard the streaking and to clean the glass again with Bon Ami before gilding the lower lines. This procedure is practical only for plain, burnished gilding. The correct method of gilding such jobs when there are outlines or varnished centers is described in the section on matte effects, page 50.

Small wrinkles in the gold are to be expected and are no cause for concern. They will be smoothed out when the gild is rubbed down with cotton. Hairline cracks resulting from these small wrinkles ordinarily are not patched. However, numerous large wrinkles do require excessive patching and should be avoided as much as possible. When a piece of leaf goes onto the glass badly wrinkled, it is sometimes possible to straighten it by carefully running more size under it, starting the flow just beyond the edge of the leaf and gradually working the size brush across the top. You can help the leaf to straighten by pulling on a corner with a fingertip, using very gentle pressure. However, it won't be possible to straighten the wrinkled leaf if any portion of the glass under the leaf is dry. Once more, keep this cardinal principle in mind: *A smooth gild is obtained by maintaining a generous flow of size on the glass.* This is best described as a flowing *sheet* of size, not rivulets of size.

## Rubbing Down the Gild

As soon as the gild is completely dry, the loose leaf and the wrinkles are removed by rubbing with cotton (Figure 19). At this stage the gild is very delicate. To prevent scratching the gold off the glass, use only clean-fiber, pure cotton that is free of seed and plant pieces. While sterile cotton packages have been preferred by many, high-quality cotton quilt batting is less expensive and often less coarse then sterile cotton. It can be found at yard goods and fabric stores. Use a big wad of clean, new cotton, and make sure that it is embedded with no foreign particles that would leave nice, long scratches in the gild. The cotton can be used for cleaning glass afterward.

Make sure that there are no wet patches in the gild before doing any rubbing. The wet places show more plainly from the outside and will appear as dull spots, whereas the leaf acquires a mirror finish as it dries. If you try to wipe across such wet spots, you will not only wipe off the leaf in those areas, but you may also wipe off some of the dry leaf with the moisture picked up on the cotton.

Rub over the leaf very lightly at first so that it won't be scratched by the particles of gold that will be picked up by the cotton. Use long, diagonal strokes, rubbing in a direction that will tend to close the laps rather

**Figure 19.** Rubbing off loose gold with cotton. Arrow shows proper direction of strokes.

than pull them open (Figure 19). After the first light once-over, which will remove most of the loose leaf, shake the particles of gold out of the cotton and go over the inscription again with circular strokes to smooth out all wrinkles. This time you can use a little more pressure, but still not too much.

This operation is often referred to as burnishing. This is an unfortunate term, for it conveys a wrong impression of what you are trying to do at this stage. It is true that the leaf can be brought to a higher luster by hard rubbing, but it is neither necessary nor desirable to do so at this time. The second application of size will bring the leaf to the desired luster.

## Second Gild

No matter how carefully the first gilding is done, there will always be some holes or cracks. These must be patched by sizing the inscription a second time and applying small pieces of leaf over them. Water size is flowed over the entire inscription, not just over the holes, and should be applied in a veritable flood. This second application of size will take away much of the cloudiness seen in the leaf after the first gilding and will bring it to a high luster. The second application of size, therefore, must not be omitted, even if there is comparatively little patching to be done.

The same mixture of size used for the first gild can be used for the second application, or it can be diluted by adding half again as much water. This will make removal of excess leaf a little easier, but not always easy enough to warrant dilution. Occasionally it may be useful to dilute the size for the second gild usually to stretching the batch of size so that a new batch will not have to be made to complete the job. The size must not be diluted when gilding with silver or palladium leaf.

Since there will be fewer pieces of leaf to apply, this time you can cover a larger area at one time than you can for the first gilding. Work with a very wet size brush to avoid scratching the gild. It is also important to keep the size brush free of dried gelatin particles and other foreign matter that might scratch the gild. Flow the size over the gild with as little pressure

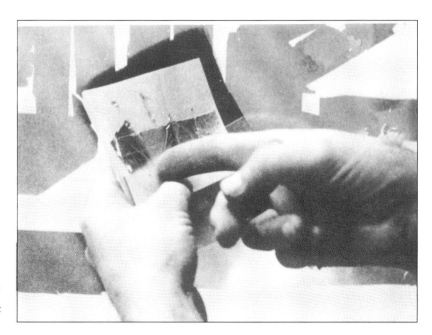

as possible so as not to lift the first gild. After thoroughly wetting the leaf, apply a second portion of size by running the brush across the glass just above the gilded area, thereby flooding the inscription thoroughly. Inscriptions that consist of more than one line of lettering should be sized in vertical sections extending all the way to the bottom in order to avoid streaking the lower portions.

Ordinarily the leaf laid during the first gild should not lift with the second application of size as long as these precautions are observed. If lifting should occur, check the following possibilities:

(1) The glass wasn't cleaned thoroughly enough. Wax or silicone may be on the glass.

(2) The size used for the first gild was too weak. A common cause of this trouble is undissolved gelatin. Remember to keep the size pail in motion while heating the size. See page 14. Don't use size left over from a previous day.

(3) The water used for the size and/or for cleaning the glass contained impurities. Use distilled water.

(4) Conditions are too humid. You might have this problem when working in an unheated store during cold, rainy weather, for instance. The first layer of gelatin doesn't dry sufficiently to permit the second application. Using a hair dryer may help under these conditions, but it is better to let the job stand until the humidity decreases. The condition is especially likely to occur when gilding with silver leaf: since silver leaf is thicker than gold, the imprisoned gelatin layer dries more slowly.

If you are satisfied that the trouble doesn't derive from insufficient cleaning, you can usually save the gild just by letting the job stand overnight, in order for the gelatin layer to harden sufficiently for a second careful application of size. To solve the problem of impure water, remake the size, apply it carefully, and let it dry. This may save part of the first gild and allow the extensive patching of a second gild.

**Figure 21.** Applying a small piece of leaf to cover a crack.

To patch holes, small pieces of leaf are cut from the book with the fingernail in this manner: Fold back a third or a half of a page at a time, cut the leaf lengthwise as previously described, then with light pressure cut the piece of leaf crosswise into four or five smaller pieces, using the back of the fingernail so that the fingertip won't come in contact with the leaf (Figure 20). Be alert to opportunities to use one big piece of leaf to cover a long crack or several small holes close together in one operation. At first you may find it difficult to pick up these small pieces of leaf with the tip (Figure 21). Be sure to charge the tip quite strongly and to give the tip a twist before trying to lift the piece of leaf.

Every little hairline crack in the gild shows very prominently from the inside of the window. Many of these will be so small that they won't need to be patched, as they are not nearly as visible on the outside. After a little experience, you will learn which cracks need patching and which can be neglected. When in doubt, go outside to examine the gild and mark those holes which need to be covered with a grease pencil. You can also tack a piece of black paper over the inscription on the outside, and then see which holes show up from the inside and therefore need patching.

On small inscriptions, consisting of just three or four leaves, you may find that it saves time to apply a solid second gild rather than patch with small pieces, especially if holes are numerous. A solid second gild is also advisable when using a poor grade of gold with an abnormally large number of imperfections. This leads to the maxim that, in glass gilding work, the best materials are also the cheapest.

While you are waiting for the second gild to dry, you can utilize the time to advantage by cleaning glass at the bottom of the window to get rid of the streaks of size and by wiping up the pools of size and loose leaf from the floor around the job. You can also mix the backing paint and get brushes ready.

When the second gild is completely dry, the inscription is again rubbed down with cotton. This time you can rub more vigorously to smooth the gild completely, for the second application of size renders the gild far less delicate.

At this point, you may wish to give the gild a third wash to increase the luster to some extent, although this wash will not increase the luster as much as the wash between the first and second gild. Probably the principal benefit of the third wash will be that large, patched places, which up to now have received only a single application of size, will be brought to approximately the same luster as the surrounding areas. (Large holes can be patched during the first gild. Their presence in any number after the first gild is an indication of poor gilding technique.)

A third wash will help harden the gelatin and make removing excess leaf somewhat more difficult. Some sign painters use a third wash only for jobs that contain large areas of burnished leaf. Make your own comparison and see for yourself if the extra wash is justified.

Plain hot water is usually employed for a third wash, although some prefer to dilute and reheat the size for this purpose. If plain water is to be used, make sure that the original size is strong enough to withstand this treatment, and don't dilute the size for the second gild. If these precautions are followed, the third wetting will add to the hardening action of the gelatin and will, naturally, make removing the excess leaf somewhat more difficult.

**Backing Up**    If you are working from a pounce pattern, it can now be applied in reverse on top of the leaf (on the inside of the window). It is a good plan to make a final check for straightness before pouncing. Also look over each letter to see if there is a little holiday near the edge of the gild. If the pattern can be shifted slightly without compromising the other letters, the holiday may fall outside the letter.

When you are satisfied that the pattern is in the best possible position, you can proceed to pounce it, using whatever color of powder that will show up best under the conditions. Usually a dark pounce will be a better choice. At times lighting conditions may be such that neither light nor dark powder will show satisfactorily. In such cases, an auxiliary light of some kind might be useful if placed quite close to the glass and to the left of the working area. A clamp-on socket with a 75-watt flood lamp is handy as it can be clamped onto a window frame, a nearby door, or a stepladder.

This time, don't dab the pounce bag on the pattern; simply rub it over the perforations. You will find that the roughness of the perforations on the reverse side of the pattern will scrape off powder in sufficient quantity to make a visible transfer, and you will avoid getting a heavy deposit that might cause ragged edges by mixing with the backing paint.

If you are working from a grease-pencil layout, it will be necessary to scratch top and bottom guidelines in the leaf at this stage (Figure 22). Due to the parallax effect of the thickness of the glass, you cannot hope to get an even line of lettering by following the guidelines marked on the outside of the window. A good tool for scratching guidelines is a sewing needle held in a pin vise or some similar handle. Try to make the scratches very fine, so that they won't be too noticeable at the tops and bottoms of round letters that extend above and below the line. You might even interrupt the scratch lines where they pass through the round letters, although lining them up might prove to be difficult.

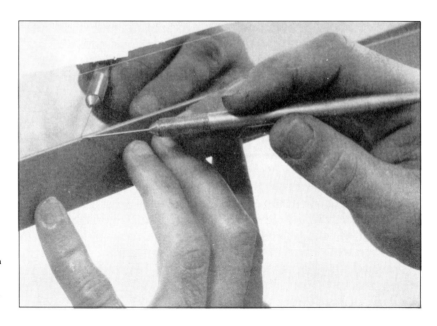

**Figure 22.** Scratching lines in the gild with a sewing needle held in a pin vise. This is necessary when working from a grease pencil layout.

Scratching the guidelines is done against a yardstick or other straightedge held flat against the glass. The straightedge needs to be placed in position carefully; it must not be allowed to slip while the lines are being scratched or the gild will be damaged. A strip of masking tape applied lengthwise on the underside of the straightedge will help prevent it from slipping.

Another method of making guidelines (suggested by E.R. Cole of Charleston, WV) is to snap lines on top of the leaf using blue chalk and strong thread to provide a fine line with good visibility.

Choosing the right paint for backing up is a matter of great importance, perhaps the single most important item of the entire job. A backing paint must work well in the brush, dry quickly, and be hard enough to withstand the scrubbing necessary to clean off the excess leaf. Although many materials have been used for backing up, that which has proved to be the most satisfactory for most gilders over a long period of years is a mixture of japan color and rubbing varnish.

Japan color is pure pigment, ground in a japan varnish base. It is good for backing-up and other delicate work, because it is more finely ground than pigments ground in oil. It can also be mixed into any type of varnish or lacquer. Different colors of japan vary in toughness. The most commonly used color for backing up is black—either lampblack or dropblack (King Cole Black was pre-mixed with varnish, but has been discontinued). Black is not actually as tough as some other colors. Chrome yellow is very tough, dries fast, and has good working properties. It can be used on most work, especially for work combining outline shades. If for some reason the backing paint ought to be a dark color, for instance if the lettering is to be finished with only a black shade, a small amount of japan black added to the yellow will darken it sufficiently. Many prefer to back up with chrome green, which is also tougher than black. It is a good substitute when chrome yellow is not available, but it is a mixture of chrome yellow and Prussian blue and therefore only intermediate in toughness.

Among current choices of varnish for mixing backing paint is *Chromatic Quick Rubbing Varnish*. Personal experimentation has indicated that Chromatic is the toughest presently available. In combination with chrome yellow japan color, it makes a backing paint that will not chip when scrubbed vigorously with Bon Ami twenty minutes after being applied, under normal temperature and humidity conditions. Even more important is that after twenty minutes it is possible to work with another color or varnish on top of the backing paint without picking it up. There are many other rubbing varnishes that will provide the necessary toughness. Among those worthy of mention is *Ronan Quick Rubbing*. Many other brands of varnish will pick up when subsequent layers are applied since they are self-solvent by nature and therefore need more time to cure and sometimes never cure at all. Be wary of synthetic or urethane-based rubbing varnish.

Japan colors are not readily available in tubes anymore, but the half-pint cans currently available can be used successfully. One must be certain to thoroughly mix the contents before each use. Stirring, not shaking, at regular intervals keeps the paint from solidifying and makes it mix better with the varnish. Sometimes the particles mixed in the paint will need to be strained, particularly when dropblack is used. (A grainy appearance may also be an indication of synthetic rubbing varnish, however.) It might save time to discard that batch and start fresh: time is more valuable than a can of paint.

Mix the backing paint with a large portion of varnish (two to four times as much varnish as color). A smaller proportion of varnish makes a paint that dries more quickly when the job is rushed; a larger proportion of varnish makes a paint that is tougher and works better in the brush.

It is important to obtain a smooth mixture. First add a small amount of varnish to break up the japan color, and add more varnish when the mixture is smooth. The paint must be strained if it contains pieces of dried color or other foreign matter. Lumps of any kind in the backing paint will cause ragged or feathered edges, and the high spots will catch when the excess leaf is cleaned off, leaving holes in the gild.

The backing paint must be just thin enough to work freely in the brush. It will usually be the right consistency when first mixed, without thinning, but, after you have worked for a while, the paint will gum up. It can then be thinned by adding turpentine very sparingly. Sometimes a smoother mixture can be obtained by adding one part Florence japan varnish or quick gold size in place of one part quick rubbing varnish. *Commonwealth* seems to be the only brand of Florence japan readily available. Some sign painters have had success with the addition of a very small amount of flow extender, such as *Edge*. Since there is some oil in the extender, contamination is possible, and therefore this too should be used in very small amounts.

One other material worthy of mention for backing up is *StaZon* neon black-out paint. It dries rapidly, and excess leaf can be cleaned off about as soon as you have cleaned your brush. StaZon is not as tough as a japan color mixture, however, and long-term durability is questionable. Although it is manageable in the brush, it is stiff and must be thinned repeatedly with special benzol-based thinner. The thinner can also be used for cleaning the brush, but it is a harsh chemical that dries out the hairs and causes them to break off easily. (StaZon should never be used for a black shade, as it will turn gray in sunshine and lift off the glass.)

The best brushes for glass work are the French, brown camel-hair quills that are not too short. Sable, ox hair and gray quills are stiff and scratchy and often produce feather edges, although they are better suited for use with StaZon and plain varnish lines described elsewhere. Usually a well broken-in brush works better for backing up than a new brush. This does not mean to use one that you intended to throw away. Used truck-lettering brushes are good to transfer over as a backing-up brush.

Do not flood the brush with color, but fill it well to avoid weak edges in the paint. A feather edge, which tapers off to nothing, chips easily when the leaf is scrubbed off and becomes ragged as a consequence. This can be avoided if the backing paint contains a lot of varnish. A heavy deposit of powder on the glass also encourages ragged edges. If you have been careless about pouncing the pattern and have gotten a heavy deposit of powder, blow some of it off before backing up.

Take your time during the backing-up operation; tell yourself, "This is something that is not meant to be done fast." This attitude relieves tension, of course, and actually gets the work done sooner. If the backing-up is done well, with patience, the job will have a finished appearance, no matter what else is done to it. It is of utmost importance to do a good job, since once the leaf is cleaned off, you cannot correct errors with any success.

Make yourself comfortable for the backing-up operation. Don't submit to having the sun beating in your face. Lower an awning or tape a piece of paper over the glass outside to provide shade. (The pattern can be used for this). Sit whenever possible on something that will place you at a comfortable height. A box built just for sitting and standing, measuring 7 1/2 in. x 15 in. x 22 1/2 in. and providing three equally graded steps is well worth the bother of carrying to the job. For high work, standing on the box is more comfortable than on the lower steps of a stepladder; however, a short stepladder often provides a comfortable stool.

The most practical way to work on glass is with a mahl stick. The leaf is delicate and must not be touched with the hands, and the glass must be kept clean. Consequently it is not practical to work by using the left hand as a rest, as on bench work. In these days, most young sign painters are trained at the bench, and the thought of learning to use a mahl stick comes as something of a shock. However, you will never be successful in leaf work unless you learn the mahl stick technique. The only work that you are likely to be able to do without a mahl stick is either a small, single line of copy or an inscription of extremely large letters.

You can buy a good ready-made mahl stick, but a superior one can be made from a straight, 1/2 in. birch dowel, cut down to 24 in. LeBlanc's mahl stick shown in the illustrations in this book was well shellaced and had an automotive spring bushing attached to one end. A small crutch-, cane or chair-tip can also be used. The most common ready-made mahl stick available at most supply houses is made by Griffin Mfg. Co. and is quite suitable for most uses. It can be assembled in either two or three sections depending on the particular job and, when disassembled, will fit well in most kits.

The following method of using a mahl stick was developed as a result of lettering a great many office doors. To letter these, you frequently need to stand on your step box, and there is no good place to put the paint unless you can hold it in your left hand. A favorite trick is to hold both a folded paper cup and the mahl stick in the left hand. The cup has to be

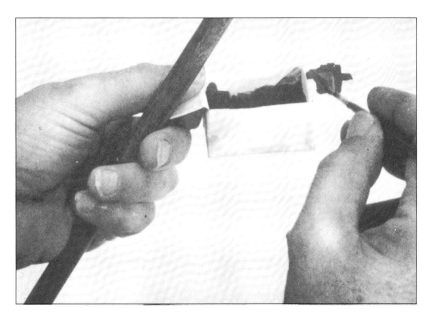

**Figure 23.** Using a paper cup as a brush palette.

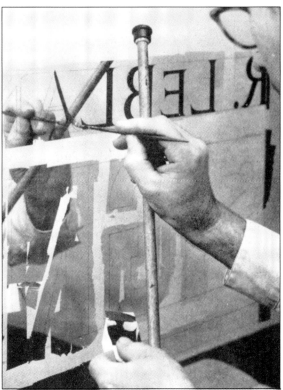

**Figure 24.** Backing up.

folded very neatly so that it won't come apart in your hand. Use only good rag-content paper, either envelopes or paper cut to that size. If your work orders are printed on lightweight card stock of good rag content, old ones cut to the size of a #10 envelope work very well. The cup is held by one flap between the thumb and forefinger; the mahl stick, by the other three fingers. The other flap of the paper cup serves as a brush palette (Figures 23 and 24). This may take several days of practice to become comfortable, but the freedom that it affords is well worth the effort. Details for making paper cups will be found in Chapter 10.

It is also possible to hold a 3-ounce paper bathroom cup with a small palette under it as well. The cup is held between the thumb and forefinger, while the bottom of the cup and the palette rest on the mahl stick, which is held with the other three fingers. Use only plain paper cups, as waxed or plastic ones will contaminate your paint. Bathroom cups also come with a handy dispenser for use in the shop and are small enough that a good supply fits in the kit.

The actual operation of backing up is no different from any other kind of brush lettering on a smooth, slick surface, except that it is done backward (Figures 24, 25, and 26). If you are accustomed to doing window lettering backward with paint, you should have no trouble doing it in gold leaf. If lettering backward is new to you, it may be advisable for you to work only with accurately drawn pounce patterns until you have fixed in your mind which way the "N"s and the "S"s go. Correct letter spacing may also be a bit trying at first and should always be of concern, as it is easy to lose perspective when working in reverse.

Should you make a mistake or an imperfect stroke while backing up, the paint can be wiped off with cotton moistened with turpentine or naphtha. If this is done gently, the gild will not be damaged. The smear left by the turpentine can be removed with clean, dry cotton. Allow the spot to dry a minute or so before painting over it again.

An advantage of working on glass is the ease with which clean, square corners can be made by extending the brush strokes past the terminals and trimming them later with a single-edge razor blade. This applies not only to vertical strokes, as in the letters I, H, K, etc., but also to the horizontal strokes of letters like E, F, and L, and to the terminals of such round letters as C, J, S, and others. Some care must be exercised to preserve the letter spacing. For example, a letter E must be made to come quite close to the letter that follows, so that the space won't be too wide after the terminals of the E have been trimmed (Figures 26 and 27). This method of extending and trimming terminals is especially useful when the lettering is being done in outline only, for it is difficult to make clean corners with an outlining brush. The outline strokes can be extended and trimmed not only outside the letters but also on the inside corners (Figure 28).

Trimming with the razor blade can be done either before or after cleaning off the excess leaf. When done before, the pattern marks on the glass may be of assistance, but, in general, a more accurate trimming job can be done after the leaf has been cleaned off. However, it will be necessary to go over the work with cotton and Bon Ami a second time to clean off the little streaks of gold that are always left by the razor blade (Figure 29).

You will find it necessary to make the razor blade cuts in a direction *away from the letter*, as the backing paint is likely to chip at the corner if you try to trim toward the letter. The proper position of the razor blade is illustrated in Figure 28.

A new razor blade should be used for this work, and it should be discarded as soon as it develops nicks and begins to leave streaks of paint. For this work you may prefer stainless, not blue, Gem or Persona blades.

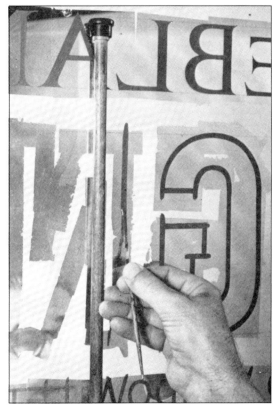

**Figure 25.** Use of the mahl stick for striping long lines.

**Figure 26.** Terminals of plain lettering can be extended past the corners, to be trimmed later with a razor blade.

**Figure 27.** Trimming terminals of small lettering. Here the three terminals of the letter E are being trimmed with one stroke.

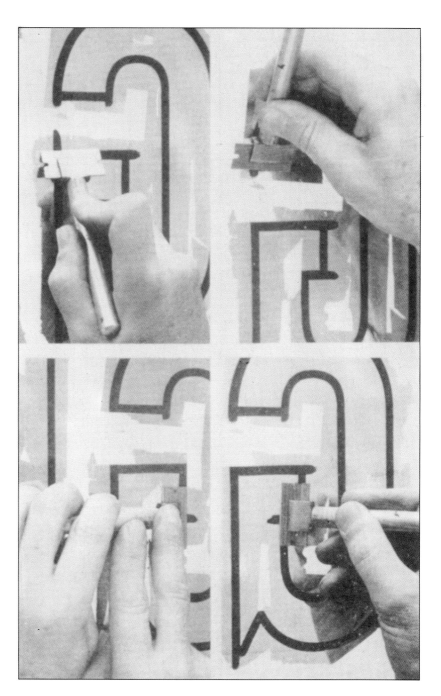

**Figure 28.** Various positions of the razor blade when trimming terminals. The cuts must always be made *away* from the letter.

While they are more expensive than most and somewhat harder to find, they have a good, straight edge and don't skip near the corners.

A good handle for holding the razor blade is a great aid to doing accurate work. The holder pictured in Figure 30 is like the "old favorite" Grifhold variety, now available from Fine Gold Lettering in Harbor City, CA, and is very good and sturdy. Some sign painters file the jaws slightly to ensure an even fit of the blade, or add masking tape to the jaws to keep the blade from slipping under some circumstances.

**Figure 29.** Above: before trimming. Below: after trimming.

When trimming in tight places that are too narrow to accommodate the full width of the blade, it is possible to trim with just a corner. This is done by lifting the other corner just slightly and applying enough pressure to bend the blade so that it is in contact with the glass across only part of its width (Figure 30). It is more convenient and much safer, however, to provide yourself with a tool to hold small pieces broken off the full blade. The Grifhold pin vise No. 44, pictured in Figure 31, is excellent for this purpose.

A word of caution about breaking razor blades is in order. This can be a dangerous operation. You can do it safely by sticking a piece of masking tape on one side of the blade; this will prevent little pieces of the blade from flying into your eyes when you break the blade with your fingers or a pair of pliers (Figure 32). The masking tape also provides a convenient means for keeping the pieces together safely and handy for use. It is advisable to make up a quantity of broken pieces in the shop rather than doing so on the job.

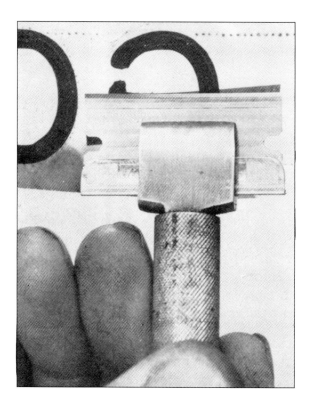

**Figure 30.** Trimming in a tight place by applying pressure on one corner of the blade.

## Making Perfect Lines and Circles

Because leaf on glass can be scratched with a suitable tool drawn against a straightedge, stripes can be made much more perfectly than is possible by striping with a brush. A good tool for making such scratches is a quill handle with the end cut off sharp and square and whittled down to about a sixteenth of an inch in diameter. (This can be done most easily in a pencil sharpener.) Wet the wood in your mouth just before you start to scratch the gold, and keep wetting at intervals along the line so that the wood is kept moist. Hold the tool perpendicular to the glass as you draw it along the straightedge, and apply quite a bit of pressure to ensure a clean line.

It may be necessary to repeat the process two or three times in order to obtain a scratch of even width for the full length of the line. Be sure that the straightedge does not slip. This operation is best done as a two-man job so that the straightedge can be held firmly at both ends; an alternative is to tape a piece of cardboard or plastic to the glass at one end to rest the straightedge against and prevent it from slipping down.

The leaf is scratched away from both sides of the stripe, and the area of gold between the scratches is backed up with clear rubbing varnish. The varnish may overlap into the scratch marks, so the brush work is not an exacting operation. After cleaning off the excess leaf, you will have a beautiful, even line.

A method that is particularly useful for producing clean, even circles is to hold a scratching point in a compass. It is necessary to provide a firm support for the stationary leg of the compass; a piece of thin plastic taped to the glass in the center of the circle works well. Use a compass, not a piece of string, and a good compass at that. Make sure it won't slip, or you will never succeed in making the ends meet. A circle scoring tool (as

**Figure 31.** Using a small piece of razor blade held in a pin vise for trimming in tight places.

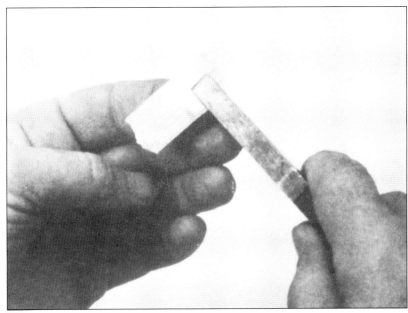

**Figure 32.** Breaking a razor blade with a pair of pliers. A piece of masking tape stuck on the underside of the blade will prevent small pieces from flying and will hold them together until they are needed.

mentioned in Chapter 10) is also handy for scoring circles, particularly when making numerous concentric circles. Ellipses can be made in the same way by taping an ellipsograph or similar tool to the glass.

These operations have to be done with quite a bit of care and skill. They are not intended to be time savers; they are methods to achieve a superior job. The extra pains are justified when a good, clean line is the result.

## Cleaning Off the Excess Leaf

You should have no trouble at this stage if the glass was thoroughly cleaned before starting the job, the water size was prepared properly, and a good backing paint was used. The leaf should clean off readily and without any

**Figure 33.** Cleaning off excess leaf. Use Bon Ami to make removing the leaf easier.

chipping of the backing paint. Use water and friction–very little water and a lot of friction.

Bon Ami can safely be used in cleaning off the leaf easily. You will find that the more quickly you get the leaf off the glass, the less chance there will be of chipping the backing paint. Take a good-sized wad of cotton or a small natural sponge, saturate it with water, and then squeeze it out just to the point that it is not dripping. (Do not wring it as dry as possible.) Rub up a little Bon Ami from the cake with the wet cotton and scrub the inscription until the leaf just begins to be worn away (Figure 33). Do a small section about six inches square at a time. Immediately, before the Bon Ami has a chance to dry, rub hard with dry cotton. The leaf should rub right off. If some small patches of gold remain when the glass has been wiped dry, repeat the operation, but avoid going over the same area too many times. Too much water on the glass can creep under the inscription and lift it.

Readers accustomed to cleaning off leaf with plain water, without using abrasives of any kind, may think this method exceedingly harsh and hesitate to try it for fear of chipping the backing paint. Bon Ami has been used successfully for many years by many gilders with definite time savings. If the backing paint chips, the paint is probably at fault. The backing paint may chip just as readily even if Bon Ami isn't used, because of the extra rubbing that is needed for complete removal of the leaf. You may also be using too little varnish, or thinning too much, or not using satisfactory materials. StaZon will chip most readily under any circumstances.

Make sure that every last trace of leaf is cleaned off. There is nothing that looks as sloppy as a gold job that has tiny specks of leaf in the outlines, shade or varnish. Inspect the job from a position in which some light-colored area can be seen reflected in the glass so that any small, remaining specks of leaf will show up. Better yet, inspect from the outside (Figure 34).

Removing the leaf is easiest when it is done soon after gilding.

**Figure 34.** Appearance of the burnished leaf work from the front, after cleaning off the excess leaf.

Gelatin hardens considerably as it stands, making the leaf more difficult to rub off. Normally you will not have too much trouble if the gild stands overnight, but you should avoid allowing two or more days to elapse before cleaning off the leaf. Not only will more scrubbing be required, but also the backing paint will become more brittle and will chip more easily than when it is fresh and in a more flexible condition.

## Finishing the Job

Frequently leaf lettering is completed without ornamentation, that is, as plain, burnished gold without outlines or shades. On these jobs the only additional operation is to pencil varnish the backs of the letters to protect them when the windows are washed. But in most burnished gold leaf jobs, you will want to add an outline or a shade. Just a little color, even black, against the gold makes for a more professional and complete-looking job.

If a shade is decided upon, it will most often be done in black. Prussian blue can also be used for shading, or any other color that appeals to the sign painter or is appropriate for the customer. The technique of shading letters is shown in Figure 35. However, black is not often used for outlining, except when it is done in the manner described in the section below "Outlines Versus Shading," because it is difficult to judge the width of black outline from the inside of the window. A transparent color is therefore preferable for outlining, and for this purpose Prussian blue is the outstanding favorite. Prussian blue is almost as dark as black when seen from the outside, but from the inside it is quite transparent, and outlining can be done with comparative ease (Figure 36). Prussian blue sets off either gold or silver very well and it is a long-lasting pigment when pure.

A black shade on burnished gold lettering is most practical. When you wish to emphasize a caption, run a thin, black outline at the top of the lettering and along the sides opposing the shade (Figure 37), but give the subordinate copy only a shade. A black shade against gold lettering produces a three-dimensional effect and therefore should vary according to the size of the lettering.

Your good judgment should be your guide in executing a shade of appropriate thickness for the size of the lettering. Variations in shading and

41

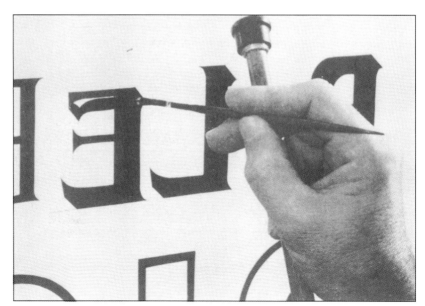

**Figure 35.** Shading with black. A guideline has been pencilled across the bottom of the letters to keep the width of the shade uniform.

**Figure 36.** Outlining with Prussian blue.

outlining, such as drop, split, and blended shades or even double outlines or shades, can be very effective with leaf and are only limited to the length of your imagination. Colors such as red can be made opaque by using a powder puff to the back with aluminum powder after the paint acquires a tack. Aluminum will also reflect light through the color and make it appear brighter. This treatment also makes a tougher, more durable job and can be used on any application. Shading or outlining can be done with either oil colors or japan colors *except* when Prussian blue is used. For Prussian blue, oil color is better. However, many oil colors currently available are synthetic and extended to the point that they are unsuitable for use on fine glass work. They will fade early or peel, and some experimentation should be employed to find a suitable brand. *Winsor & Newton Selected List Colours* and *Chromatic*

**Figure 37.** Combination shade and outline.

**Figure 38.** Three common types of ornamentation. On the last two letters, a combination of outline and shade retains the heft provided by a shade while the complete outline secures extra protection for the gold.

*Pictorial Oil Colors* can be used with good results. For outlining or shading, mix them with a half-and-half mixture of quick rubbing varnish and turpentine. A little linseed oil or flow extender can be added to make the brush marks flow out better. Transparent lettering enamels can be used, although they may dissolve the backing paint.

## Outlines Versus Shading

It must be kept in mind that it takes less time to add a shade than to outline lettering on glass when the outlining is done on the inside after the lettering itself is completed. Outlining letters from the back calls for considerable skill in order to keep the outline uniform, and small departures from uniformity in the width of the outline are quite noticeable. (This doesn't apply to outlining done before gilding, which is a comparatively easy operation.) Shading, on the other hand, doesn't require as much care; if the shade varies a little in width from letter to letter, it won't be criticized.

However, outlining does have some advantages over shading that should be considered. One of these is that outlined lettering will last longer, since the leaf portion of the letter is protected on all sides by an additional coat of paint. Outlined lettering is also easier to read at night when the lettering shows only in silhouette against a lighted interior. The outline doesn't distort the shape of the letter nearly as much as a shade does under these conditions (Figure 38).

Shading, on the other hand, is good treatment when curtains, drapes or venetian blinds are hung behind the inscription. Shading gives the lettering the necessary heft to make it legible against distracting backgrounds of this sort. Another good treatment for use against distracting backgrounds is to make the inscription inside a solid or stippled panel.

## Varnishing

A satisfactory varnish to be used as a final protective coating is not easily found, for the requirements are exacting. The old-time long-oil varnishes, made with natural gums, were excellent in their ability to stick to glass, but they have become extinct. Phenolic resins and urethanes, which comprise the bulk of the spar varnishes available today, are not as durable on glass. They don't seem to be able to resist the sun's action, which breaks down the resin and causes the varnish to flake off, sometimes pulling off the entire inscription with it. Chromatic Clear Overcoat Varnish, an alkyd resin varnish, provides durability and works well in the brush. It can be thinned with turpentine, mineral spirits, or flow extender, and dries slowly enough that it usually does not affect backing paint. The longer curing time required by this product should be taken into account when giving washing instructions to the customer, who should wait ten days to two weeks before cleaning the window.

Varnish that crawls on the back of lettering is common and aggravating. Crawling is likely to occur when varnishing is delayed until several days after the application of the last paint layer. Cold glass also increases the tendency of varnish to crawl, as do certain combinations of oil and varnish used in the backing paint. The most effective cure is to give the back of the lettering a light turpentine wash before varnishing. Wipe over the back of the lettering with a wad of cotton saturated in turpentine and squeezed dry. Allow about five minutes or so for the turpentine to dry, wipe off the turpentine smear with damp cotton and then wipe dry. Since varnish only crawls on thoroughly dry paint films, particularly those left several days, there is little danger of the turpentine picking up the paint.

Varnish is applied with a quill over the backs of the letters and extended slightly beyond the edges. Don't make this varnish outline beyond the letters too wide. Besides being unsightly, a wide varnish outline actually affords less protection than a narrow one, for the strongest part of the varnish film is the little ridge that builds up along the edge. This ridge should occur as close to the edges of the letters as possible. Ideally, the ridge should be the only part of the varnish which outlines the letters. Perhaps you may have noticed old window lettering on which the varnish was almost completely worn away, but this ridge was still intact, standing alone away from the letters. The same principle also applies to other lettering, which will be more durable when a natural ridge is laid on with a brush than if it is applied by spray, roller, or screen printing.

Flow on the varnish as liberally as possible without creating runs. If a few sags develop behind the letters, they won't be objectionable. With any varnish, the job will wear longer if a thick film is applied. An extra measure of protection is assured if the varnish is applied in its thickest form, as close to package consistency as is brushable.

It is important that windows not be washed too soon after the lettering is completed so that the varnish will have time to cure hard enough to withstand lifting. Allow at least a week in warm weather, longer in cold weather. A good precaution is to attach a warning sticker to newly completed jobs or to older lettering that has been revarnished (Figure 39).

**Figure 39.** Sample warning label for newly gilded windows.

Even with such precautions, there is occasionally some damage to the varnish during the first few washes, for a good varnish remains soft to some extent for quite a while after it is applied. If the chipping is not too extensive, it can be disregarded, as eventually it will stop and the lettering itself won't suffer. If the price received for a job justifies extra precautions to assure a long life, two coats of varnish might be applied: one coat of the varnish normally used, followed by a coat of rubbing varnish. Rubbing varnish dries hard in a short time and will protect the more durable varnish underneath until it has cured past its delicate period.

## Gilding Windows on Upper Stories

The method described here is applicable for any window where, for one reason or another, applying a pattern or pencil layout on the outside of the glass is not practical, such as windows on upper stories. Occasionally this situation is encountered even on ground-floor windows. In such situations, it is obviously impractical to apply a pattern or pencil layout on the inside of the glass and then gild immediately with water size, as water size can only be used on clean surfaces. A guide of some sort must be provided, however, unless you are prepared to gild a large area by guesswork and waste a lot of time and leaf.

This problem is solved by outlining the lettering in black (or some other color) prior to gilding. When the paint outlines are dry, it is a simple matter to gild inside their boundaries. (This is sometimes referred to as the European method.)

For work of this kind, a pounce pattern is advisable. If the lettering is marked out with grease pencil, pens, or other markers, it is difficult to clean off the marks thoroughly enough for water size without damaging the paint outlines. Lines that are crisp enough for outlines are not easy to mark with chalk on clean glass. For simple jobs, Stabilo pencil or washable pens

45

Figure 40. First step in executing gold lettering on upper floor windows. The lettering is outlined in black, *outside* of the pattern lines, on the inside of the glass. Corners inside the letters are completed with the brush; outside corners are trimmed with a razor blade.

can be used with some success, though they are still hard to clean off thoroughly.

The first operation is to clean the glass thoroughly, just as for any other glass gilding job. Then the pattern is applied on the inside of the glass, in reverse, and the lettering is outlined (Figure 40). Use a mixture of japan color and rubbing varnish, similar to backing paint. Don't use oil color or any slow-drying paint, as the outlines will not be able to resist the scrubbing necessary later when cleaning off the excess leaf. Do not use a flow extender or other oil, since these will make the water size crawl away from the outlines. Remember that black is not an especially tough pigment, so mix the paint with plenty of good rubbing varnish and no turpentine. Lampblack japan color is tougher than dropblack; adding yellow will keep it black, and even tougher. Work with the brush rather full so as to avoid weak edges.

Painted outlines are not considered to be part of the letter and should therefore be done outside of the pattern lines. The brush strokes can be extended past the outside corners and trimmed later with a razor blade. Corners that occur inside the letters are best completed with the brush (Figure 40). If you wish, however, you may also leave these corners to be trimmed with the razor blade, but unless they are trimmed very cleanly, they are likely to show as smudges in the gild.

By using a little care it is possible to gild over the outlines as soon as the paint is dry enough not to smear, usually about twenty minutes. Trim the outlines, and wipe the paint scrapings and the pounce powder off the glass before starting to gild (Figure 41).

Many a sign painter has been discouraged from using the outline method when, at this point, the water size crawls furiously from the paint outlines. Sometimes a particular mixture of paint will not make the size crawl, so test it first. If it does crawl, there is a simple remedy: Add four drops–no more–of household detergent to each pint of size. (Use a liquid detergent, not a lotion). Use the least amount of detergent possible up to a maximum of four drops. This small amount of detergent will make the size flow over the paint outlines as though they weren't there! This same trick—adding detergent—is employed when gilding over varnish centers or for any similar work in which water size must be applied over paint or varnish. (A drop

**Figure 41.** Figure 40, after trimming the terminals.

**Figure 42.** Gilding inside the paint outline.

two of detergent added to water colors will also overcome their tendency to crawl on slick surfaces such as glass or metallic card.)

Don't try to pour the detergent into the size from a can; you will invariably get too much in, causing the size to lose some of its adhesive ability and to lift the painted outlines. Use a medicine dropper, such as a small prescription dropper available at drug stores. This is handy to have in the kit for other liquids as well.

Gilding the outlined letters is done as previously described. Gilding is actually much easier using the painted outlines as an exact guide for the placement of each piece of leaf (Figure 42). Do the second gild as usual, then back up the leaf inside the outlines (Figure 43). You will find that the outlines show easily through the leaf and that backing up is easier than on conventional jobs. It doesn't need to be done accurately. You need only stay within the outlines, but be sure to overlap the backing paint onto the outlines all around, or there will be holes in the letters when the excess is cleaned off.

When the backing paint is dry enough, clean off the excess leaf. You will probably find that the leaf doesn't clean off the paint outlines readily.

**Figure 43.** The leaf is backed up inside the outlines.

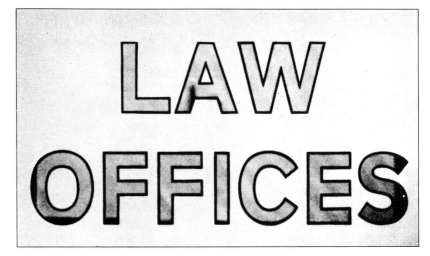

**Figure 44.** The complete job as seen from the front. (The dark areas in the O and S were caused by objects reflected in the glass when the photograph was taken.)

Don't try to clean up this little edge of gold. It isn't objectionable, and you may chip the paint outlines by trying to clean off all the gold completely. (Caution: If the entire letter wants to lift during clean up, there was too much detergent in the size.)

As soon as the leaf has been cleaned off, the job can be varnished and is then complete (Figure 44). All things considered, this method is the easiest way to do a leaf job on glass.

Ordinarily, work on upper-story windows is not done as carefully as street-level jobs, since slight imperfections in the work will not be visible from the street. It is usual to make allowance for this in charging for the work.

# 3 Matte Effects

When leaf is applied directly to glass with gelatin water size, as described in Chapter 2, the effect is burnished, that is, shiny. If, instead, the leaf is applied on top of varnish, the effect is matte, or dull. Although these two terms, burnished and matte, are well understood among sign painters, a clearer meaning will be conveyed to a customer if you use the terms *mirror finish* and *satin finish*.

The most common use for matte finishes in glass gilding is in the centers of letters, in combination with burnished outlines. Other combinations are possible, such as matte outlines around burnished centers. The use of matte finish for portions of logos and designs offers an alert sign painter a great outlet for his imagination and increases the effectiveness of his work.

Most signs can derive a great advantage from two-tone gilding. When selling gold lettering, bring these points to the attention of the customer, preferably by showing samples. For instance, when gold leaf inscription is entirely burnished, reflections of dark objects such as buildings or trees will make the lettering appear dark from certain positions. Under these conditions, matte portions in the inscription are "lighter" and will make the lettering appear bright from all directions. Of course, in locations where open sky is reflected in the glass at all viewing angles, which is often the case on upper-story windows, there is no point in using matte centers. Conversely, for upper-story jobs in which the glass catches only dark reflections, it may be proper to make the inscription entirely matte. (This is true only for upper-story windows; on street-level windows the burnished gold outline makes an important contribution of movement to the effectiveness of an inscription.) Matte areas also make an inscription more visible at night.

Matte gilding can be done in three ways. In two of these methods, clear varnish is laid on the glass with a brush, the difference being in the way the leaf is adhered. The first method is to apply the leaf directly from the book to the varnish when it has attained a whistle tack, just as in ordinary surface gilding. The other way is to apply the leaf with water size over partially dry varnish, as in conventional burnished gilding. The resulting matte finish is pretty much the same for both of these methods; the choice should be determined by the particular circumstances of the job, which will be explained as we go along. The third method, which can be objectionable under some circumstances, is the very old technique of using stale (flat) beer in place of water size. If beer is used, the result is an absolutely even matte finish, though not quite as "dead" as varnish.

Almost any kind of varnish can be used to achieve a matte effect including rubbing varnish, spar varnish, japan gold size, damar varnish, or mixtures of these. Again, the circumstances of the job will determine the choice of varnish. The determining factor is usually the drying time. For example, when a small inscription is to be surface-gilded onto tacky varnish, rubbing varnish, possibly mixed with Florence japan (usually referred to as hot mix), will set up for gilding in ten minutes or so. On a larger job, it might be more convenient to use quick gold size, perhaps *tempered* with a little slow size or spar varnish, which will hold its tack for an hour or more.

The same principle applies if gilding is to be done with water size on top of partially dry varnish. The varnish must not be completely dry; it must retain a *barely perceptible tack*. This is important. If the varnish is allowed to become hard before gilding, it will not render a nice, dull matte, but will have shiny spots. (This might be desirable for embossed effects, but not for matte finishes.) The best varnish to use is damar with a little quick rubbing varnish added as a hardener. Keep in mind that damar will absorb the dryer in the rubbing varnish and that it may have to be replenished by adding a small amount (a drop) of japan dryer. Let the solvent (turpentine) flash off and then gild as usual with water size.

Burnished portions of window inscriptions are usually done with XX deep gold (23-karat). The matte portions can be done with the same leaf for a full, rich appearance, although they are most commonly done with lemon gold (18-karat) or pale gold (16-karat), either of which yields a flashier effect and complements the burnished outlines well. For two-tone silver or white gold lettering, the matte portions are done with aluminum leaf, since the silver will tarnish in contact with varnish. White gold can be used for single gilds over damar varnish, but the varnish must be very close to dry when the white gold is applied.

Following is detailed information on procedure for various combinations of two-tone gilding.

**Two-Tone Single Gild**

In this method the varnish for the matte portions is put on first. When it has dried to a barely perceptible tack, the entire inscription is gilded using water size. That portion of the leaf lying on top of the varnish will have a matte finish, and the leaf that is directly on the clear glass will be burnished (Figure 45). This is the quickest, though not the easiest, method for executing a two-tone leaf job. It is not recommended for very small lettering or where the best workmanship is needed, because fine detail on glass is difficult to execute accurately with brush and clear varnish. For exacting work, double-gild methods are preferred.

Jobs done by this method can be done with or without a pounce pattern. Working from a pattern involves a few extra operations, but is easier and more accurate.

The pattern must be accurately drawn and accurately perforated. It is important to keep the widths of the letter strokes uniform. Otherwise there will be a noticeable variation in the widths of either the burnished outlines or the matte centers. Where roman or script styles are employed, be sure to draw the thin strokes wide enough to accommodate the matte center without crowding. The width of these strokes must be twice the width of the

**Figure 45.** Two tones of gold (burnished outlines and matte centers) with a single gild.

burnished outline plus enough left over for the matte center, which can be quite narrow in the thin strokes. It is not customary to draw the centers on the pattern, because pounce powder dots at the edges of the varnish strokes would lead to trouble.

After the glass has been thoroughly cleaned, the pattern is applied on the *inside* of the window. Be sure to make accurate registration marks, because the pattern will need to be placed in exactly the same position for backing up. This is important. Figure 46 shows a good way to make these registration marks.

If gilding is to be done on the same day, as it usually is, use a quick-drying mixture of varnish. A mixture of two parts Chromatic Quick Rubbing Varnish and one part embossing damar varnish can be safely gilded over with water size in about 15 minutes and will still yield a good matte effect after two hours. Whatever varnish is selected, remember that gilding must be done while the varnish still retains a slight tack in order to obtain an even matte finish without shiny streaks.

The center varnish should be thinned by adding turpentine, so that the brush marks and laps will flow out and reduce the tendency of the brush to skip and leave holidays. Use a good sharp brush, a little on the long side, for putting in the varnish centers. These should run right down through the middle of the letters as shown by the pounce pattern (Figure 47). It is advisable to leave a generous outline between the centers and the outside edge of the letters. Then, if the width of the outline is not quite uniform, the irregularities won't be too noticeable. You can achieve more accuracy and will find it easier to make clean corners if you work with a fairly dry brush. As you complete a short section, examine the work for holidays and unfinished terminals.

With practice, you may be able to see clear varnish against the clear glass well enough, but you might experiment on this point before going to an actual job. If you find it too difficult to see the work, you can dust the glass lightly with white pounce powder, which will give the glass a light, frosted appearance against which the varnish strokes will appear transparent and quite visible. A small amount of whiting mixed with water and applied to the glass with a rag will also give a more solid frost. Either powder or whiting must be applied before pouncing on the pattern, of course. Another

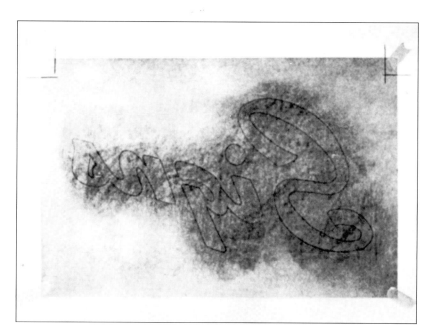

**Figure 46.** Applying the pattern to the inside of the glass. Note the registration marks on the two upper corners of the pattern.

**Figure 47.** Putting in the centers before gilding. (To show this clearly in the photograph, the glass was lightly powdered with talcum. Against this the varnish shows as transparent or dark in the photograph.)

method of making the varnish more visible is to mix a very little white pigment in the varnish. Use just enough to give it a light, cloudy appearance on the glass.

If you wish, you can extend the varnish strokes past the terminals and trim them later with a razor blade. You will have to trim them very cleanly, preferably by going over the work a second time with a new blade, or the places where the varnish was scraped off will show as cloudy areas in the burnished gold.

When the varnish is dry enough, clean off the powder and proceed with the gilding. This is done as described in Chapter 2 for simple burnished

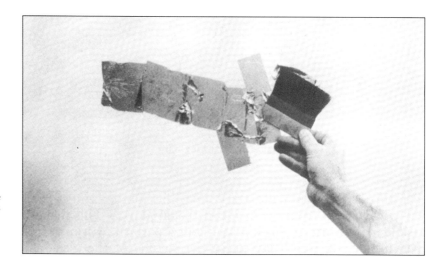

**Figure 48.** Gilding over the varnish centers. During this operation be careful not to wash off the registration marks, seen in the upper corners of the photograph.

gilding. Remember that you may want to add a few drops of detergent to each pint of size so that it will not crawl on the varnish centers.

It is possible to place the leaf by using the varnish centers as a guide, but many sign painters prefer to use a pattern pounced on the outside of the window for this stage of gilding. In either case, be sure to gild far enough to cover the burnished outlines all around the letter (Figure 48).

When the gilding is completed and ready to back up, apply the pattern again on top of the leaf. Make sure that it is in perfect registration with the first pattern so that the varnish centers will come exactly in the middle of the letter strokes. The backing paint should be solid inside the pounce lines (Figure 49). Do not use StaZon for this operation, as its stronger solvent base will result in an uneven matte.

At this stage you will notice that the matte centers show clearly in the gild from the inside of the window. This makes it possible to do work of this kind without a pattern, working from a pencil or chalk rough layout on the outside of the glass as your guide for the varnish centers. When working this way, without a pattern, backing-up is accomplished most accurately by going around the matte centers with an outlining brush, then filling in.

You may occasionally detect holidays in the matte portions of a letter during the backing-up operation. It isn't too late to fix these. Simply cut in around the holiday with backing paint, leaving that portion bare. Then, after the excess leaf has been cleaned off of the entire inscription, dab a little varnish over the spot, and, when it is tacky, apply new leaf and cover with backing paint. This will correct a small holiday nicely, which is usually all that one will likely miss during initial varnishing.

Clean the excess leaf as described for burnished gilding in Chapter 2. At this stage the job can be considered complete except for varnishing, without a shade or outline (Figure 50). This type of job is the kind done almost exclusively in the fashionable sections of many big cities (New York in particular). When well done, with good, even mattes, it looks rich and smart. If you wish, you can add a simple black shade, as in Figure 51 (popular in Philadelphia). It is not unusual to add an outline, known as *Boston style*, to a two-tone job done in this manner (Figure 52), described in the next section.

**Figure 49.** Backing up.

**Figure 50.** Clean off the excess leaf and the job is done!

**Figure 51.** The same job with a black shade added.

**Figure 52.** Boston Style— two-tone single gild with black outlines. The black outline is done first, then the varnish center is added. Finally, gold is applied over all.

An interesting variation of the two-tone method is achieved by doing the job in lemon or pale gold instead of the usual XX deep gold. The work is done exactly the same way except for the substitution of leaf. Lettering done in lemon or pale gold is very effective when shaded with Prussian blue. For a silvery appearance, the work can also be done with white gold; in this case, the center varnish should be almost dry when the gold is applied to avoid tarnishing the silver content in the white gold.

It is also possible to use this method for a job with burnished XX gold outlines and lemon or pale gold matte centers with a small additional operation. Begin as described above, but instead of allowing the center varnish to dry, surface gild the letters with lemon or pale gold as soon as the varnish has become tacky. (Do not use damar varnish, which will not hold a tack long enough to gild.) Apply water size and gild again, all over, with XX gold and follow with a solid back-up. Small inscriptions are done this way just as quickly as by the straight method, since the time required to apply the lemon leaf in the centers is no longer than you would normally wait before it would be safe to gild over the bare centers with water size.

**Two-Tone Single Gild with Black Outlines (Boston Style)**

This is by far the easiest method of doing a matte center in an inscription (Figure 52). It is an excellent method for those who wish to confine themselves to only a few techniques.

The pattern is applied only once, so the registration problem is eliminated. The work is done in the manner described for inscriptions on upper-story windows with the addition of matte center. The glass is cleaned, the pattern is applied on the inside of the glass, and the lettering is outlined with black or another suitable color (Figure 53). The varnish centers are painted in as soon as outlines are completed (Figure 54). Gilding can be done as soon as the varnish is sufficiently dry, which takes about fifteen minutes if rubbing varnish is used (Figure 55). When the backing paint is dry, the excess leaf cleaned off, and the lettering varnished, the job is completed. The most difficult part of the job is outlining the letters. The outlines provide a perfect guide for placement of the center varnish and for gilding. Backing-up is not fussy, requiring only that you stay within the outlines (Figure 56).

This type of job is used quite often for upper-story windows, as is

**Figure 53.** Outlining the lettering from a pattern applied to the inside of the glass. No registration marks are necessary, as the pattern is applied only once. Outlining is done *outside* of the pattern lines.

**Figure 54.** Putting in the varnish centers.

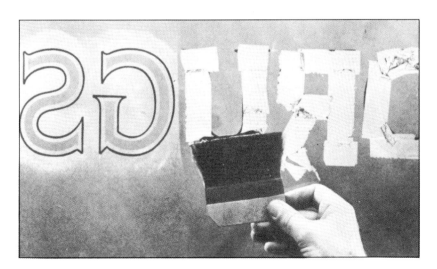

**Figure 55.** Gilding.

the simpler version without matte centers. The method is also useful for street-level jobs when you wish to do a matte center without too many complications. A fair-sized job can easily be completed in one day, including varnishing.

**Double Outlines**

Occasionally you may want to embellish a two-tone single gild with more than a simple outline in black or any other color. The additional color is very effective in areas where pedestrian traffic is heavy and close observation of the sign is likely. One option is to add a second outline of a different color outside the original outline (Figure 57). When the first (inner) outline is black, it should be kept narrow and the colored outline made somewhat wider. When both outlines are colors, they should be kept the same width. Two tones of one color can be very effective when the darker tone is painted first, closest to the gild.

Outlining with the second color is the last operation before varnishing. The paint should be applied over the entire back of each letter for a neat appearance from the inside of the window. The additional coat of paint on the letters also assures a long-lasting job, especially if a good oil color is used. Chromatic Pictorial Oil Colors, mixed to a transparent consistency in alkyd Chromatic Clear Overcoat Varnish, work well. A second application of the same transparent color will give the darker tint appearance needed close to the letter. A good alkyd resin *lettering enamel* (not bulletin enamel) such as *Chromatic* or *One-Shot* can be used for the color outlines, but remember not to skip the final varnish.

The colors most commonly used for the second outline are red and green, but any color can be effective when applied with some imagination. Appropriate colors might be those used to identify the business elsewhere, the colors used on the building, or even the ones chosen for its furnishings. Pictorial oil colors can be mixed for a fairly accurate match without appearing muddy or streaked.

A double outline is a good treatment to use in restaurants, barber shops, beauty parlors and similar places where windows are likely to steam over in cold weather or, for whatever reason, the lettering needs to be particularly durable. A further measure of protection for lettering subjected to severe conditions is to apply a layer of heavy aluminum leaf on top of the final coat of outline color. For this additional treatment, use oil color with oil gold size added for the color outline (instead of the overcoat varnish) and gild with the aluminum leaf the following day, when the paint has achieved proper tack.

**Split Shades**

Two-tone or split shades can be painted in the same manner as double outlines. As in double outlines, the first shade next to the letter should be a darker color than the outer shade. An additional treatment is to start with the black outline, use two colors of shade, and add a black line "stop" at the outer edge of the second shade.

To achieve an old-fashioned look, *transparent* shade colors can be blended for a three-dimensional effect. After the shades are dry, brush a dark color (asphaltum, umber brown, or gray) on the backs of the shades at an angle in the areas to be the "low spots" of the shades. Then *blend* in white over the dark color as well as the rest of the shade. This will give a stronger dimensional effect to both the shade and the letter itself (Figure 58).

**Figure 56.** Backing up. It is only necessary to keep within the black outlines which show prominently through the gold.

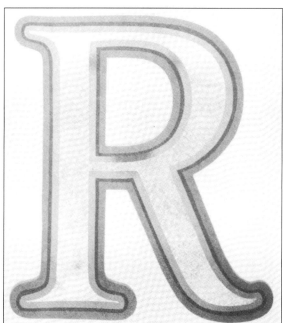

**Figure 57.** Two-tone single gild (Boston Style) with double outline.

While this is complicated to explain, it is quite simple to do and was a very popular effect during the Art Nouveau/Art Deco period. This and other more complicated effects are most easily learned under supervision of someone who is familiar with the techniques. Techniques for gilding, hand lettering and other processes are frequently shared and demonstrated at national or regional sign painting meetings held in recent years by the Letterheads.

**Convex Effects**   A convex appearance can be executed in gold leaf in a number of ways, but a variation of the Boston style is a comparatively simple method to use. This particular technique is done extensively in Chicago, which has much fine gold glass work.

The work is begun as for the Boston Style; the glass is cleaned, the pattern is applied on the inside, and the lettering is outlined in black or

59

a.

b.

c.

d.

**Figure 58.** Split-blended shade process as demonstrated by Mark Oatis, Denver, CO. (a) Fill in transparent colors between completed letter and shade stop line. Let dry. (b) Lay in colors for dimensional effect (such as black, gray and white seen here). (c) Blend them together while wet to soften transitions between them and add dimension. (d) Finished letter from the front shows full dimension.

**Figure 59.** Convex letters, done with two tones of gold (single gild) inside a black outline.

other suitable color. The outline should be kept quite narrow for this style of treatment.

When the outline paint is dry enough to withstand being brushed over with varnish, put in the highlight portions of the convex effect with the usual matte center varnish (Figure 59). The portions to be done in varnish are usually the tops and right sides of the letter strokes. Figure 60 will serve

Gold Leaf Techniques/*Matte Effects*

*(mirror-image lettering)*
ABCDEFGHIJK
LMNOPQRSTU
VWXYZ.,:;? 1234
567890&AB CD

**Figure 60.** Shows placement of the matte varnish (the shaded areas) in executing convex lettering.

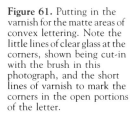

**Figure 61.** Putting in the varnish for the matte areas of convex lettering. Note the little lines of clear glass at the corners, shown being cut-in with the brush in this photograph, and the short lines of varnish to mark the corners in the open portions of the letter.

as a guide for the placement of the varnish. It is not advisable to indicate the placement of the varnish highlights on a pounce pattern because a pounce line on the edge of varnish strokes is troublesome, especially if the varnish is thinned with turpentine as suggested in the section on two-tone single gilds. The procedure is no more difficult than making ordinary matte centers (Figure 61), and the varnish highlights can be placed entirely by eye after you have studied where they are to go according to the letter plate. Other letter styles can easily be adapted to the convex effect for a letter which really "pops" off the glass.

The job is completed as is other work of this type, that is, gilding inside the outlines, backing-up the solid areas, cleaning off the excess leaf, and varnishing.

Convex effects can also be done in four tones of gold by those who have a flair for more complicated treatments. A possible combination could be: tops of letter strokes in pale gold (16K) matte finish; right sides, burnished pale gold; left sides, XX (23K) burnished gold; and bottoms of strokes, XX (23K) matte gold glazed with burnt umber. (A *glaze* is a mixture of just enough pigment into the varnish to make a very pale, transparent tint.) The sequence of operations would be: apply matte varnish to the tops of strokes only; gild the letter solid with pale gold (lemon gold or others could be used as well); back up the tops and right sides; clean off excess leaf; apply matte varnish tinted with burnt umber to bottoms of strokes; gild solid with XX gold; back up; clean off excess leaf; and varnish.

Convex lettering can be done without the black outline, if desired. The procedure would be as described as for two-tone single gilds, except that varnish would be applied as a highlight as shown in the letter plate, Figure 60, instead of in the centers of the letters. The use of black outlines makes the job much simpler, however.

**Gilding Large Inscriptions**

When gilding with water size over painted outlines or varnished centers, it is important to prevent the water size from collecting in drops on the top edges of the paint or varnish. If water size does collect into drops, it may work underneath and separate the paint or varnish film from the glass. An inscription consisting of only a single line of lettering presents no problem, for lifting is prevented merely by maintaining a solid flow of size over the work until the leaf has been applied. This prevents the formation of drops.

When there is more than one line of lettering, one under the other, the bottom lines are in danger of being damaged by the size that runs down the window if the top line is gilded before the rest of the inscription. The best solution is to gild in vertical sections, working on all the lines at once, so that the flow of size is maintained all the way to the bottom of the inscription. Outlining or applying varnish on the bottom lines first, so that these portions will be more nearly dry at the time of gilding, adds a further measure of safety on such jobs. There will be little danger of lifting during the second gild, for the dry gelatin and the leaf already laid on the letters prevent the size from working under the paint.

**Double-Gild Technique**

In the techniques that will be considered in this section, the burnished outlines and the matte centers are gilded separately. Although similar in general appearance to the single-gild method, the two-gild method produces outlines, centers and corners that are neater and more uniform, particularly for small lettering, and is preferred whenever a quality job is called for (Figure 62). The first operation will be to outline the lettering with burnished leaf. The open centers are then filled in with any of numerous treatments available, many of which are not adaptable to the single-gild method. The majority of gilders use this method when using a center treatment, as it provides a base for more than the simpler matte center.

**Figure 62.** An example of the small detail made possible by the double-gild technique with burnished outlines and matte centers.

## Making the Burnished Outline

The burnished leaf outline is considered to be part of the letter, and therefore will be made inside of the pattern lines, unlike painted outlines. In thick-and-thin styles, some judgment has to be exercised in establishing the width of the thin strokes. On thin scripts, Old English, and some delicate Roman styles, the thin strokes of the letters can consist of just a single burnished outline stroke, leaving the matte centers only for the thick strokes and possibly the serifs. A much more readable inscription will result if you can manage to make the center complete in all parts of the letter, so that the matte portions as well as the burnished portions will read as a complete letter. The center in the thin strokes can be made quite narrow, even a hair line, but will still require that the letters be drawn sufficiently wide to accommodate both outlines and the matte portion. These principles are illustrated in Figure 63.

The work is begun as for any simple, burnished leaf job. Apply the pattern on the outside of the glass, clean the glass thoroughly on the inside, gild and back up. In this case, the backing up is done in outline only (Figure 64). These outlines should be kept quite narrow to make a neat job.

On lettering up to about eight inches high, it is preferable to gild the letters solid. For larger letters, it may be practical to gild only the edges, using narrow pieces of leaf. In backing up, the outline strokes can be extended past the corners both outside and inside the letters and later trimmed with a razor blade. In trimming, remember to cut *away* from the letter so as not to chip the paint at the corner (Figure 65).

When the burnished outline is completed and the excess leaf cleaned off, you are ready to proceed with filling in the centers (Figure 66 and 67). Be sure that the backing paint is dry enough so that it won't pick up under the varnish or paint that will be used over it later. As mentioned before, it is possible for the backing paint to be dry enough to permit safe removal of the excess leaf and still be too wet for varnish to be applied over it. Usually it is safe to proceed if the backing paint is no longer tacky, but it is always safer to make a test. Choose a terminal that will be trimmed off

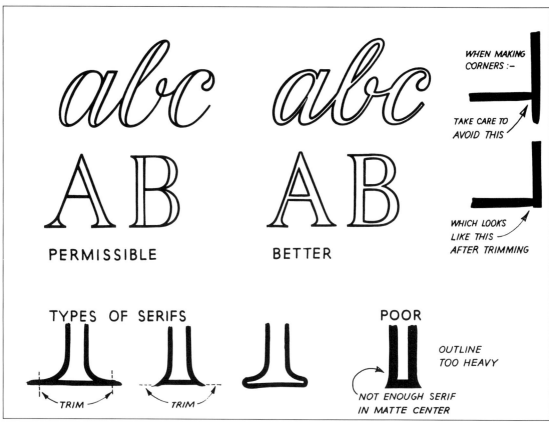

PERMISSIBLE

BETTER

WHEN MAKING CORNERS :–

TAKE CARE TO AVOID THIS

WHICH LOOKS LIKE THIS AFTER TRIMMING

TYPES OF SERIFS

TRIM

TRIM

POOR

OUTLINE TOO HEAVY

NOT ENOUGH SERIF IN MATTE CENTER

**Figure 63.** Principles of outlining lettering.

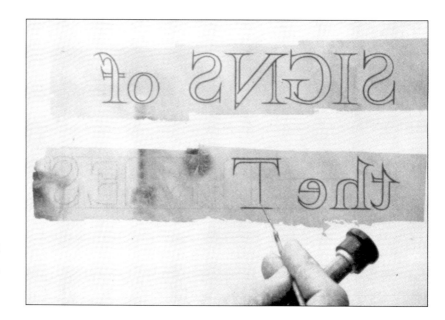

**Figure 64.** Backing up small burnished gold outlines. In this case the outlining is done inside of the pattern lines, as the outline is part of the letter.

**Figure 65.** Trimming the outlines using a small piece of razor blade held in a pin vise.

**Figure 66.** Cleaning off the excess leaf. Bon Ami can safely be used.

**Figure 67.** The completed burnished gold outline. The centers can now be filled with any of several matte leaf treatments or with a color.

**Figure 68.** Painting the centers with varnish for surface gilding with gold leaf.

and brush over the same area four or five times, not just once, to make a valid test. For more complicated effects it is advisable to coat the outlines with clear, overcoat varnish, since quick rubbing varnish is self-solvent with other varnishes of the same base.

Some possible treatments for the centers are given in the following pages. These are not the only methods possible, but merely a beginning point for the ingenious. After a little experience with these basics, you will be able to devise many more effects appropriate for a particular job or job location.

**Simple Matte Effects**

A simple matte effect can be achieved merely by filling in the centers with a suitable varnish (Figure 68) and gilding with appropriate leaf, which might be 23K, lemon or pale gold. Aluminum leaf is usually employed for the matte portions in combination with burnished outlines done in silver or white gold.

For ordinary matte centers it is customary to apply the leaf directly from the book onto the varnish while it is tacky, just as in any other type of surface-gilding work. Some prefer to allow the varnish to dry and then gild the centers with water size, which produces a more even matte finish. This might be a consideration if the matte areas are large. The surface-gilding method is much quicker and generally satisfactory. Aluminum leaf can only be applied onto tacky varnish, because it is too heavy for successful gilding with water size. In the detail that follows, it will be assumed that the surface-gilding method is to be employed.

The varnish for gilding the centers can be rubbing varnish, spar varnish, gold size, or mixtures of these, sometimes tempered with oil size. Use whatever will set up and be ready for gilding in a convenient length of time. The varnish should be thinned a little with turpentine to make it flow smoothly and free from laps. Brushing the varnish on is not an exacting operation. It is only necessary to completely fill the open area in the letters without going outside the outlines.

Leaf should be applied while the varnish has a fairly strong tack,

**Figure 69.** Applying leaf to the centers. Note that the overlap of leaves is made to occur between letters. The leaf is applied with an upward rolling motion.

generally as soon as you can touch the surface lightly with a knuckle without having the varnish come away on your skin. Remember that in this gilding you are not trying to achieve a high burnish, only a dull finish. If the leaf is drowned in the varnish a little at this point, it will not matter. It is a good plan to brush on little test patches of varnish here and there outside the inscription as you go along so that you can determine the tackiness of the varnish without messing up the letters.

A few precautions need to be observed when applying leaf to the centers. The leaf is applied with an upward, rolling motion of the book (Figure 69). The leaf must be kept tightly stretched as it is being applied so as to avoid wrinkling. Once the leaf is started, don't allow the book to slip on the glass, or the leaf will break and you will have a nice long crack that will not be easy to patch. Finally, don't allow the rouged paper to come in contact with the varnish, for the rouge will stick and make the joint between leaves noticeable. It is good practice to avoid joining leaves within the letters, even if it means wasting a little leaf.

After you have gilded a portion of the inscription, go over the gilding with the ball of a finger or the heel of the hand (which leaves no fingerprint) to press the leaf firmly into the varnish (Figure 70). This operation is particularly necessary when rubbing varnish is used for size, since it doesn't develop as strong a tack as other varnishes.

When the entire inscription has been gilded, you can rub off the loose leaf with clean dry cotton (Figure 71) or a badger hair shaving brush. When gold size is used for the center, the leaf can be burnished to produce a pattern, such as plaid or engine turning, which will attract attention with its unusual light-gathering capabilities. The merits of this burnish are illustrated in the section on surface gilding in Chapter 6 and in particular in Figure 90.

Usually a certain amount of leaf will stick to the glass here and there around the letters. This can be cleaned off by going over the inscription with slightly dampened cotton, then wiping dry. Now examine for holidays.

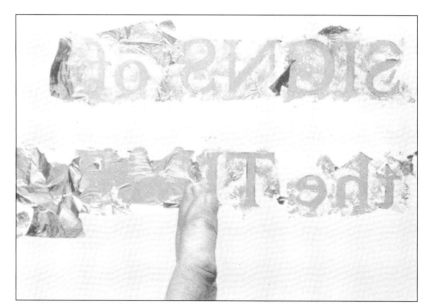

Figure 70. Pressing the leaf into the varnish with a rolling motion of the finger. The ball of the thumb can also be used.

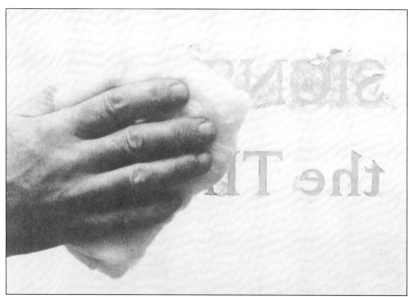

Figure 71. Wiping off the loose gold with cotton. Gold that still adheres to the glass will be wiped off afterward with damp cotton.

There will usually be a few. Those that result from imperfections in the leaf and which still have varnish in them can be patched by pressing small pieces of leaf into them. Any holidays that occur in the varnish coating will need to be patched by dabbing a little more varnish over them (Figure 72) and applying leaf when the varnish becomes tacky. This type of patching is acceptable only for very small holidays. Large areas should be caught during the initial operation, for large patches will show as different streaks in the matte.

A second method for applying matte centers, mentioned in Chapter 2, is to use stale beer instead of varnish. As mentioned earlier, some locations might not be suitable for this, as the area around the work can smell like a brewery while you are working. It does, however, yield the most even matte

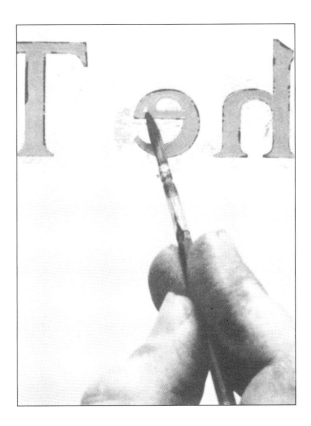

**Figure 72.** Filling in a holiday by applying more varnish.

possible. It is particularly useful for gilding large areas, where unevenness is a problem when the varnish does not flow out well. Beer also makes the overlapping of leaves virtually unnoticeable. While the matte effect is not quite as dull as it is with varnish, it is still quite attractive.

To gild with beer, allow a can or bottle to go stale (flat) to the point that no bubbles are left. Since you don't actually want the beer to spoil, open it and then refrigerate it while it goes flat. That is all the preparation that is necessary. Using the beer size, "water gild" the centers of the outlined letters. A second gild with beer size is tricky, so try to gild solid in one attempt. If patching becomes necessary, do not re-size with the beer size; instead, breathe heavily on the area to re-wet it enough to gild. Back the center up in the usual manner, using the outlines as a guide, and clean up as you would for any water gild.

If the lettering is to have an outline or a shade, the same color should be painted solid over the backs of the letters, no matter what method was used for the matte. When using varnish, this can be done immediately after gilding the centers; on a beer size, after the backing paint is dry. If the lettering on varnish centers is to be left plain, without outline or shade, it is customary to back up the centers with the same paint used when backing up the outlines (Figure 73). This will cover any hairline cracks in the gild that might not show from outside, but which are plainly visible from the inside.

Backing up the centers of varnish matte is chiefly for the sake of making a nice appearance on the inside; this operation can be omitted if the job is rushed, as the final varnish coating will provide ample protection for the center gilding. In such cases the final varnishing can be done immediately after gilding the centers.

69

**Figure 73.** Backing up the centers. This operation can be omitted if the job is rushed, as its purpose is merely to give the inscription a neat appearance from the inside.

**Figure 74.** A window inscription with burnished 23K gold outlines, lemon matte centers and Prussian blue outlines. This makes a very durable job. Note that the centers of the stars are abalone.

Two-tone lettering in which XX (23K) gold is used for both outlines and centers can be left plain, or, if you wish, an outline or a shade can be added. When the centers are done in lemon or pale gold, the lettering looks unfinished without an outline or shade. The combination of lemon gold and Prussian blue is especially pleasing (Figure 74). Medium chrome green also looks good with lemon or pale gold leaf, as do maroon, purple and earth tones.

**Color Centers**     Instead of applying a matte leaf to fill in the centers of lettering, a color can be used. This can be white or light tints, black, red, green, or any color under the sun. Very smart effects are produced this way. For this type of

**Figure 75.** A small decorative door piece in two tones of silver, combined with colors. Borders around the shield, ribbon, and helmet, and ornamentation around the shield, are done with silver leaf outlines and aluminum matte centers. Background of the shield is white (appears dark in the photograph in comparison to the silver). Flags, helmet plumes, chevron and ribbon are red. The entire design is approximately 8 inches high. The small lettering is ⅛ in. and has matte centers.

**Figure 76.** In this small barber pole on a window, the bands of color are separated with burnished gold outlines. Lettering is plain burnished gold.

treatment the burnished outlines should be kept narrow. The lettering shouldn't be embellished further by painted outlines or shades when the centers employ strong colors, but a shade can be an enhancement when pale tints are used.

When mixing the color to be used, make it as heavy as possible and apply a thick film so that it will not need to be stippled. Stippling may be necessary on large letters to achieve an even color, but this is difficult to do neatly in small letters. Also, the work will last longer if no stippling is done, as stippling leaves a very thin paint film. Although japan colors or lettering enamels with a little added linseed oil will also work, the best colors to use, as in all glass effects, are oil colors. For a bright effect, they can be mixed to a light transparent glaze and, when dry, water-gilded with white gold. Colored bronze powders can be used as well for a very flashy or bright color.

Pictorials and logos can be most attractive with colored centers (Figures 75 and 76). Almost any inscription on glass can be enhanced with the use of burnished gold or white gold outlines.

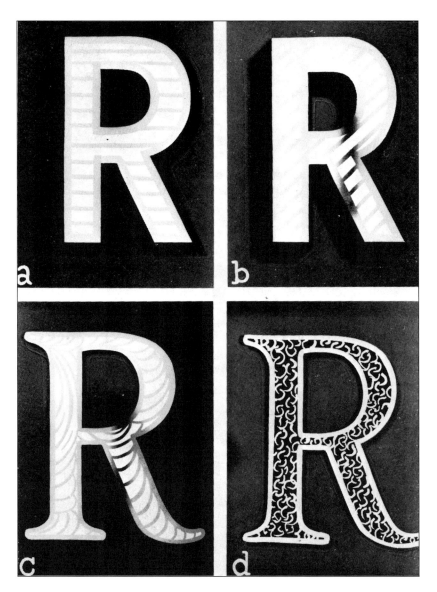

**Figure 77.** Examples of burnished gold center ornamentation. (a) Horizontal lines in burnished XX gold, XX gold matte center, Prussian blue outlines. (b) Diagonal lines of burnished XX gold, lemon matte center, black shade. (c) Burnished XX gold outline and center ornamentation, lemon matte center. (d) Burnished XX gold outline and center design, center filled in with black.

## Burnished Filigree Ornamentation

Some very startling effects can be created with filigree or burnished gold line designs inside letter centers (Figure 77). It is a good treatment to use on inscriptions that have a feature line of only a few letters and can also be used for stars, starbursts, dingbats and the like to pick up some characteristic of a logo or pictorial and to satisfy the demand for something "different." The work requires skill and time, but it is not difficult to do.

When this treatment is to be employed, the letters have to be gilded solid during the first burnished gilding, of course. The lettering is backed up in outline paint. Be sure to complete the inside corners of the outline with a brush, as it won't be possible to trim them. The pattern chosen for the centers is created in reverse with the backing paint. You can use any pattern of ornamentation that suits your fancy and your passion for complications. The example shown in Figures 78 and 79 indicates to what extremes this type of work can be carried out.

Gold Leaf Techniques/*Matte Effects*

**Figure 78.** A more ambitious job of burnished filigree center ornamentation. Centers of the flowers are XX matte gold. Balance of the centers are lemon gold over embossed damar varnish. Letters are 8 inches high.

**Figure 79.** For the center ornamentation of Figure 78, a small overall pattern was made and applied successively over the backs of the letters individually, as shown here.

After the excess leaf is cleaned off the glass, the lettering will be seen as burnished outlines with burnished line ornamentation in the centers. The centers might even be left open and the job considered complete just as it stands, consisting entirely of fine, burnished gold lines. This will create a delicate effect that might be appropriate for certain feminine shops. The open portions in the centers can also be filled in with a color or any style of matte finish. If the centers are filled in, the varnish or color employed does not need to be painted in each opening individually, of course. It is applied solid over the entire letter, although some areas could be skipped for other colors or whatever imagination brings to mind.

## Embossed Centers

Embossed centers are probably the most beautiful and striking effects possible to achieve with gold leaf. The centers have a heavy texture that will stand out from the outlines in bold relief (Figure 80). This effect is accomplished by filling the centers with embossing white damar varnish, which is a very

**Figure 80.** Embossed centers.

heavy, pale varnish that can be applied in a thick layer. It sets quickly, so that a design worked into it with a suitable tool will remain while the varnish hardens. Gilding is done with water size on top of the embossed varnish, after the varnish is dry.

Although embossing damar varnish is quite thick as purchased, it is possible to allow it to thicken even more by leaving it in an uncovered container for two or three weeks. The varnish is turpentine-based and, if thickened too much, can be thinned again. If a skin forms on the surface, it can be mixed back into the varnish, since it dissolves without leaving particles.

A little rubbing varnish mixed with the damar will cause it to dry both faster and harder. Although damar sets rapidly, it is exceedingly slow to dry, especially when it is applied in a thick film.

The varnish is laid in the centers as evenly as possible with a sable or a gray quill. In order to achieve a good relief, it should be applied in a fairly thick layer. Be careful not to let it get so thick that it runs and collects in pools at the bottoms of the letters, where it may remain wet for weeks and cause additional paint films to crack. Everyone has a tendency to apply a thicker film in the large areas of the letters than in the thin strokes. This should be avoided if possible, for where the thickness of the varnish varies, the setting time also varies, causing irregular relief when the varnish is embossed.

Too thick a varnish, collected in the outlines, can also lift the backing paint or draw it into the damar with ugly streaks. When time permits, it is advisable to go over the outlines of embossed work with clear overcoat varnish. Chromatic Clear Overcoat Varnish, an alkyd, will not be dissolved by the damar. If a thin line of clear varnish intrudes the center, it will not detract as much as streaks of backing paint in the embossing.

Damar can be stiffened considerably and its tendency to run can be reduced by adding a gel medium such as *Weber's Res-N-Gel*, a synthetic resin jelly that, when mixed with paints, reduces their tendency to run. It

Gold Leaf Techniques/*Matte Effects*

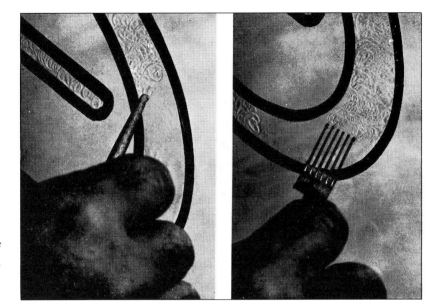

**Figure 81.** Stippling the soft damar. (a) Using a rounded end of a quill handle and little circular strokes. (b) Using a small section cut from a comb and mounted on a quill handle, especially useful for large areas.

is available through artists' supply stores. For those who have seen reference to *Balsam-of-Fir* in older publications, Res-N-Gel is the modern replacement and is easier to use, much less find. Use about two parts damar and one to two parts Res-N-Gel and add a little rubbing varnish. Air bubbles will form in this mixture when it is stirred, and although they won't settle out, they are easily broken up when the brush is paletted. This mixture is far easier to work with than straight damar and rubbing varnish and will hold the embossing better.

Embossing the soft damar can be done with a small, stiff brush (toothbrush or fitch that has been cut down), a quill handle, a notched sliver of wood, or any similar tool. Quill handles are especially handy, since a sign painter always has one in his kit. A little experimenting along this line will be fruitful. Figure 81 shows two tools, a quill handle and a section of comb, being used in a continual, scrubbing motion to create little circular strokes. A light touch is necessary so as not to scratch the backing paint in the outlines and deposit dark specks in the damar. An even, consistent motion will make it easier not to leave unembossed areas.

Embossing must be done at just the right time. Too soon, and the design will flow out again; too late, and the texture will have sharp edges and deep pits that will be difficult to gild. Varnish is in the ideal condition when it will still flow slightly, so that the little hills and valleys are nicely rounded off without causing the design to disappear completely. If you do start to emboss too soon, you can still redo areas that have flowed out.

You might plan the operation so that you leave approximately the same amount of time for filling in as you do to emboss each letter. Above all, make sure that you can emboss at least as fast as you fill in; otherwise the damar will set ahead of you. Especially avoid embossing too late. After every few letters, make sizeable test patches of varnish as thick as has been used in the actual letters.

Gilding the centers cannot be done on the same day they are

**Figure 82.** Gilding over the damar centers. This must be done with water size.

embossed. Wait until the following day at least or, better yet, two or three days. Gilding is done with water size (Figure 82). (Add detergent if the size crawls from the varnish.) Don't attempt to varnish and surface gild for a matte effect, as the varnish will re-wet the damar and the embossing will flow out. The embossed damar yields a somewhat burnished appearance with water size but beer size can be used for a matte effect. Lemon or pale gold can be used. Don't color the centers, or the embossing won't show. Either palladium or white gold must be used for silver lettering, as aluminum cannot be gilded with water size.

After the first gild, you will most likely have quite a lot of holes where the leaf hasn't gotten down to the bottom of the depressions in the varnish. A generally successful method of filling these is to apply a solid second gild and then patch the most severe holes with small additional pieces. It is especially important to maintain a generous flow of size over the work when gilding these embossed centers. Don't be in too much of a hurry to rub the gild with cotton when it is completed. Those little depressions contain pockets of water size that take quite a while to dry, and it is difficult to determine by inspection whether they are still wet. After completing the gild, take a coffee break.

It may occur to you to try surface gilding from the book on top of the soft damar. Don't try it. You will make a mess. Damar is a surface-drying type of varnish that doesn't develop a good gilding tack.

Back up embossed centers with a liberal application of chrome yellow japan mixed with plenty of good rubbing varnish, not turpentine (Figure 83). The excess leaf can be cleaned off as soon as the backing paint is set to the point that it won't smear. Bon Ami is to be used for cleaning off the leaf, but should be rubbed somewhat more gently than normal for this operation, since the damar will still be soft enough that you could knock off the high spots. It is best to clean off the leaf as soon as possible after backing it up, as this is when it can be cleaned off most easily.

Old-time instructions for gilding over damar centers caution against

Gold Leaf Techniques/*Matte Effects*

**Figure 83.** Backing up the centers.

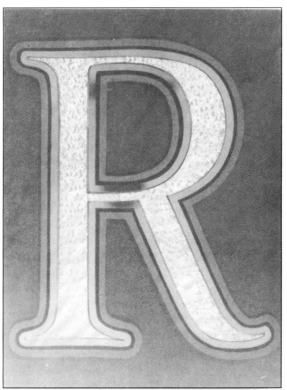

**Figure 84.** In this example of embossed center work, a hairline of burnt sienna separates the center gilding from the burnished outline. This was put in before applying the damar varnish. Center is lemon gold. The letter is finished with double outlines of black and red.

using a quick-drying material as a backing paint on top of the damar for fear of causing cracks. Cracks are most likely to be a problem when an exceptionally thick layer of damar, as thick as a sixteenth of an inch, is piled up for a heavy relief. Res-N-Gel added to the varnish eliminates this problem even for fairly heavy reliefs.

Another method to protect an embossed finish against cracking

**Figure 85.** A fair-sized window inscription with embossed lemon centers and finished with Prussian blue outlines and shades. Letters are 6, 4½ and 2½ inches high.

and damage from window washers is to add a layer of heavy aluminum leaf. Back up the embossed area with spar or overcoat varnish and, when the varnish is tacky, stick on heavy aluminum leaf. Varnish can be used for this operation because the layers of leaf and gelatin already applied will prevent it from penetrating and softening the damar. Allowing the damar to dry an extra day or two before gilding the centers also provides an extra measure of safety.

If an outline or shade is added to the inscription after the centers are completed (Figure 85), the color should be painted solid over the backs of the letters, as on other work. If the lettering is to be left plain, the final varnishing can be done as soon as the backing paint is sufficiently dry. Overcoat varnish is not likely to lift the damar, as it has a mild solvent base.

Pearl and other materials are frequently used with embossed centers for added color and texture. When mixed with rubbing varnish (and possibly a small amount of dryer, as mentioned above), damar is a good adhesive for pieces of mother-of-pearl, abalone shell, lace, silk, jewels, watch crystals, glass smalts, coins, wallpaper, or any number of materials to add color and texture to the inscription. Damar serves well for this purpose because it dries slowly enough that you can force out all bubbles and position the piece correctly.

While the embossing process is long, it may appear more complicated than it really is. This is only because so many details have been included here to keep you out of trouble. Embossed centers make beautiful jobs, and the satisfaction that you will derive from them will repay your efforts many times. One or two of them around town will also increase your reputation quite a bit.

# 4 Special Techniques

**Gilding on Clear Plastic**

It may occur to some readers that gilding could be done on clear plastic sheet, just as on glass, and it can — with a few precautions. The coating of wax and/or adhesive from the sheet's protective paper must be removed before gilding with either water size or varnish size. The plastic must be cleaned very thoroughly with detergent. Acrylic should be given a final wiping with denatured alcohol; polycarbonate should be cleaned with polycarbonate thinner. Bon Ami or any other type of abrasive cleaners cannot be used, as these would scratch and frost the plastic.

Any of the techniques used in glass gilding can be employed on plastic in the same manner as on glass. Excess leaf must be removed with plain water and, of course, no Bon Ami after gilding with water size. The leaf will be easiest to remove as soon after gilding as practical. Trimming with a razor blade should be kept to a minimum. To keep from scratching the plastic, hold the blade almost parallel to the surface. Only a blade without a handle will get close enough to the surface to allow this.

Static is likely to be a severe problem when working on plastic, particularly on polycarbonates. If possible, work in a humid atmosphere. A cool-vapor humidifier placed near the work or misting the opposite side of the plastic with water will overcome the problem.

**Painted Panels**

Ordinary painted window signs, in which large areas of glass are painted out with a background color, are familiar work for most sign painters. Such signs may include top valances, bottom strips, and panels of various shapes centered in the window, with either stippled or transparent letters or backgrounds. They have the advantage of being readable at night when the interior of the store is lighted.

These painted panels may also employ gold. The simplest example is the conventional black panel with plain burnished gold lettering and border, perhaps incorporating any of the variations for matte centers described in Chapter 3. Other dark background colors might be employed, such as blue, green, maroon, purple, or various shades of brown, or transparent stippled backgrounds can be used for night visibility. Considerable variety is possible: The background can be opaque and the lettering transparent, or the other way around, or both can be transparent or both opaque. Gold might be used in outline only, with the letter centers of one color and a background of a different color.

Even if the use of gold is confined to a thin outline, the job is nevertheless a gold job and far above the class of ordinary painted signs. Think of such jobs not as painted work with gold outlines, but rather as gold jobs with a painted background, and you will have the right frame of mind for selling this type of work.

Any gold work in a painted panel should be done first. When the gold work is completed, you can proceed to fill in the colors. The color combination to be employed will determine whether to fill in the letters or the background first. Obviously, common sense tells us to do the opaque portions first and then apply the stippling paint over all.

Oil colors continue to be the best choice for glass work, either for solid or for transparent effects. They cover well, work easily in the brush, and set slowly, which is necessary for stippling. Linseed oil is still one of the best materials for durability on glass. For good workability and proper drying, add paste colors to a mixture of half raw linseed oil and half overcoat clear or spar varnish. If there are large areas to stipple, use less varnish to maintain the workability of the paint for a longer period.

The purpose of stippling is to eliminate brush marks and to distribute the paint evenly. If the letters are large, transparent centers will need to be stippled, but the process can be omitted in small letters if the color is carefully brushed. Stippling small letters is a tedious job, usually done with a small fitch, and leaves many paint smears around the letters that will have to be wiped up before the background can be filled in. If the background is filled in first, leaving the letters clear, the stippling can be applied over all. On the other hand, when letters painted are solid in some strong color such as red or blue, and the background is to be stippled white or some light tint, fill in the letters first, cover them with the background color, and then stipple the remaining area. This will hide any slight unevenness in the letters. Devices of this kind eliminate a lot of work in doing painted panels.

Transparent backgrounds are always stippled when they are white, any pastel color, or red. Most other colors can be opaque, using two coats if necessary. It is possible to stipple some dark colors, such as blue, for a transparent effect but it is difficult to do smoothly and should be avoided if possible.

For best results in stippling, mix the paint heavy, but brush it out thin, as evenly as possible on the glass. Large areas of color are best applied with a fitch *cutter,* preferably a *double thick* one. The actual stippling is done with a cloth-covered absorbent pad. Use three or four thicknesses of absorbent cheesecloth, lint-free cotton, or velvet wrapped around a wad of cotton made to size for the job. The ends of the cloth are gathered in a bunch at the back of the pad and secured with masking tape or string (Figure 86). Don't make the pad too tight and hard, or it will produce a spotty stipple. On the other hand, if it is made too soft and limp, there is a possibility that wrinkles may develop in the cheesecloth cover and leave a pattern in the paint film. Women's sanitary napkins make excellent pre-made stippling pads and are capable of soaking up an enormous amount of paint before they become useless.

Paint rollers, particularly the foam type, can be used both to apply paint and to leave a stippled finish on glass, but need to be used with caution. Too many passes with a roller can lift the lettering and make such a mess

**Figure 86.** Stippling a background.

that you will need to start the entire job over. Rollers do not allow for as much control as do pads, which are easily created in different sizes to cover uneven shapes.

The paint must be stippled while it is good and wet, before it has a chance to set up. The stippling pad should be loaded with a small amount of paint to avoid stippling the first portion more lightly than the rest. Dab a little paint on the pad with the brush and work it in by stippling a few times on a piece of scrap paper or an area of empty glass. Stipple the glass with a succession of soft, overlapping taps, lifting the pad only a couple of inches or so between each tap. Work in vertical lines from bottom to top. For an extra smooth job, go over the area twice, the second time using the pad very gently with a random technique, rather than in straight lines.

Panels in which both the lettering and the background must be stippled present difficulties. An example of such a case is the familiar red background with white letters. The safest procedure is to fill in and stipple the background first, wait for it to dry, then paint and stipple the white over all. Several stippling pads of different sizes will be needed for the background; large pads for the open areas and small ones to get in between the letters. Getting a background color into a letter can never be completely avoided. When this happens, immediately smear the color with your finger into a thin film, and let it set up. It can then be wiped off easily and cleanly with a small wad of damp cotton.

When a panel with stippling on both lettering and background must be completed on the same day, it will be necessary to apply the lighter

81

color first; otherwise, in the case of the red background with white letters, it would be impossible to paint the letters without picking up pink smears from the wet background. Any over-stippling with the first color can be wiped off, but the second color cannot be removed and must therefore be stippled with extreme care. A more modern method is to mask the letters with masking paper, stipple the background, and then stipple the lettering after the background is dry and the mask removed. A roller is efficient over masking paper.

After stippling a large area, you will find that the pad becomes loaded with paint and that you cannot obtain a smooth stipple. If you are not a conservationist, the simple thing to do is to discard the loaded pad and make a fresh one. The pad can be coaxed into extra service when necessary by opening it and turning the cotton around.

A stippled paint film won't last as long as one that is solid. This is partly because the stippling process leaves a surface full of little dimples in the paint. These spots soon wear down to bare glass and provide numerous edges from which further deterioration progresses rapidly. If you want stippled backgrounds to last a long time, they should be varnished; Chromatic Clear Overcoat Varnish works well for this purpose. Still better is to apply two coats of background color, both stippled. A two-coat job will last not twice, but three or four times as long as a single coat. This is because the second coat of paint fills up the little depressions in the first coat and results in a paint film that is much more uniform in thickness. A two-coat job won't fade as quickly as a one-coat job, either.

Usually it is not considered necessary to varnish over opaque backgrounds, because the paint film will usually be thick enough to assure many years of service (assuming that a good oil color is used). A pencil line of varnish should be applied along the exposed edge, however, just as in varnished lettering, since paint films on glass will begin to deteriorate first at the edges.

The two principal enemies of paint films on glass are sun (ultraviolet rays) and heat. Signs on sunny windows, on windows near heat vents or radiators, or in the path of any hot air flow, don't last nearly as long as similar work done on cool, shaded windows. In such conditions the thickness of the paint film is not as big a factor as the premature drying out of the oils that hold the paint on the glass. On windows in particularly harsh situations, a generous amount of castor oil yields good results. The paint will stay wet for weeks, but ordinarily no one goes near a window after the background has been painted. Resin varnishes also last well under such conditions, since these materials have been formulated for baking.

## Marble Backgrounds

Imitation marble backgrounds were popular around the turn of the century and are an effective way to add interest and color to a stippled background. Surface gilding on marble actually is less brilliant and less attractive than a glass gild. A gilded imitation marble panel will appear to have more movement, yet will look like an expensive marble plaque when hung in lobbies, etc. Marbling on a small area of a glass window sign will also enhance a line of copy or a logo.

The technique is relatively simple to produce, taking little more time than two-color stippling. The first step, after the lettering has been

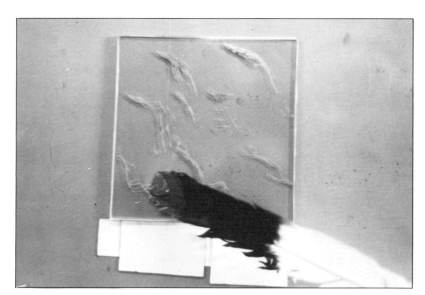

**Figure 87.** Veining technique using a turkey feather for a "marble" background.

**Figure 88.** Completed marble background panel.

done, is to put in the veining, which gives the marble appearance. Lines of solid color are made behind the lettering by using a feather dipped in oil color mixed in varnish (Figure 87). A feather (especially turkey or goose quill) gives the unique shape required for the marble look. The most common technique is to draw the feather across the panel diagonally in a twisting motion to simulate the character of the veins.

The background color (in Figure 88, white) is then lightly stippled over the veins to soften the edges and add an aura of color around them. This can be done with a bulletin or soft fitch dipped in the background color just enough to add a touch of color on the hairs. When this is dry, the entire background is coated and stippled to finish the panel. The example shown (Figure 88) has emerald green veins with a background of aura blending to white.

83

## Enhanced Transparent Backgrounds

A background color that has been mixed to a very light tint can be used as a very transparent finish to create an unusual background. Particularly on small panels, the background behind the lettering should be very transparent. After the alkyd varnish is dry, apply quick gold size. When it comes to gilding tack, apply aluminum leaf or variegated leaf for an interesting effect. Use water size to gild white gold over the back of the transparent background, and you will have a bright background. Use damar varnish and apply wrinkled aluminum foil to get a reflective "facet" effect that attracts much attention. With a little imagination, you will find many other possibilities for this technique.

## Black Backgrounds

Large areas of black paint on windows with a sunny exposure are likely to heat the glass excessively and cause it to break. On a clear winter's day, when the outside temperature stands at around 20 degrees, a black background window can be so hot that you will find it impossible to keep a hand on it. Such unusual heating is due to the black's absorption of infrared rays. Dark colors that transmit infrared freely will not cause the glass to heat to the same extent. Prussian blue can be substituted successfully for black on backgrounds. To make it darker, add a little orange, which will also kill the purple hue so characteristic of Prussian blue.

It is also possible to use a quite transparent glaze made by adding a very little black to a considerable amount of varnish and linseed oil, followed by a full coat of Prussian blue. This makes a more neutral background than the Prussian blue alone and is less likely to cause breakage.

Windows that never receive sun, or do so only in early morning or late afternoon, can more safely be painted with black.

## Glass Gilding in Cold Weather

It must be kept in mind that not only water size, but also paint and varnish, dry much more slowly on cold surfaces and that under cold weather conditions it becomes necessary to allow more time for materials to dry. In wintry weather, sitting in a sunny window may be quite comfortable, and it is easy to overlook the fact that the glass may be quite cold.

When the glass is so cold that water size freezes on it, it is impossible to attempt any glass gilding: gold will obviously not adhere to frozen size. Mixing alcohol in the size, as is often suggested, is of little help, since the alcohol evaporates quickly and the size still freezes.

When the problem is not freezing, but merely slow drying, a hair dryer may speed up the work on small inscriptions. Be careful not to heat an area too much, or the glass may crack from stress between the hot and the cold areas. On larger gilded areas an ordinary electric fan can be used. Silver and other heavy leaves take an exceptionally long time, sometimes hours, to dry on cold windows, making their use in cold weather impractical. Static build-up in the book of leaf causes the leaf to adhere to the rouged paper and is a common annoyance during winter months, especially when working in overheated and overdry interiors. It is generated by stroking the gilding tip through the hair and is then transferred to the book. It will be considerably reduced if you keep your hair in an oily condition. Static is also generated by sliding the leaf off the rouged paper; therefore, lifting the leaf off the book, rather than sliding it off, will also prevent static build-up to some extent. Static can be discharged by breathing heavily on top of each page of the book just before lifting the page.

In cold weather, backing paint must be allowed extra drying time before cleaning off the excess leaf, or applying either more paint or varnish over it. Adding a dryer such as cobalt dryer or japan dryer does not help. The dryer will only speed the setting of the top of the backing paint; it will not allow you to clean up with much success. Neon block-out paint can be used as a backing paint with some success in cold weather, most notably for backing up small inscriptions that must be done quickly. Remember not to use it for outlines or shades, as it deteriorates rapidly under ultraviolet rays. However, the best method of dealing with cold weather is to take a break and wait.

When varnish is used for surface gilding in matte centers on cold glass, it behaves in a peculiar manner. It sets up and loses its tack rapidly, so that making it take leaf is difficult. However, it dries slowly and may cause the leaf to crack or drown when paint is applied over it. On cold glass a slow-drying varnish thinned down well with turpentine will better retain a tack. A thin film will dry more uniformly. Also, to be safe, do not back up surface-gilded matte centers on the same day. Water size may actually be a better choice for the matte center, although freezing may be a problem.

One final point about gilding during the winter months is that more time must be allowed to elapse before the window is washed. Whereas a window may be washed ten days to two weeks after gilding in warmer weather, a three-week wait may be necessary in the winter.

## Gilding with Silver Leaf

Many sign painters feel that silver leaf is a poor substitute for 23K gold in window inscriptions, but that it should be used with aluminum trim on windows and doors. Others, who view the window frame as part of the architecture and separate from the sign, consider gold as attractive as silver on such windows. In some applications, however, silver may be called for to complement various elements of a design or decor.

Although silver is cheaper than gold, silver lettering should be charged for at the same, if not at a higher, rate as gold as it takes even more time to do.

Since silver is difficult to work, some sign painters have preferred palladium leaf instead. There is actually little difference between the two in workability. While palladium is a little easier to lay, the extra leaf is far more difficult to clean off. In addition, the color of palladium is dark and therefore not as pleasing as silver. Since it is also the most expensive of all the leaves, a much better substitute is 12K white gold, which has a workability close to that of gold, even though the excess is slightly more difficult to clean off.

Size for silver leaf may need to be made a little stronger than for gold, depending on the thickness of the leaf. The very thin, domestic brands of silver leaf can be gilded satisfactorily with size of the same strength as used for gold, which is two No. 00 capsules per pint of size. The heavier, imported silver leaves will require two and one-half to three 00 capsules per pint of size. Don't dilute the size for the second gilding.

Cutting silver leaf in the book is made easier by rubbing up a little rouge on the fingernail. Don't waste time by cutting silver into small sections, as it is cheap enough to use full or half leaves for small areas. Gilding with full leaves is easier with silver than with gold because of its thickness.

Make special effort to obtain a smooth gild, for every little wrinkle in silver leaf will need to be patched. If the first gild contains many holes

85

and cracks it is simpler to make the second gild solid rather than to patch with small pieces. Maintaining a good flow of size on the glass is especially important. Wrinkled leaves can usually be straightened out on the glass by running additional size under them and by teasing them with the gilders tip.

When gilding with silver leaf on cold glass or in damp weather, it is wise to allow extra time before rubbing down the gild with cotton and starting the second gild. This will give the gelatin layer a chance to toughen and will minimize the danger of lifting from the second application of size.

Mix the backing paint with plenty of varnish and thin it sparingly with turpentine. When the paint becomes too heavy, it is better to add more varnish, either quick rubbing or Florence japan, to make it flow better. If possible, clean off the excess leaf soon after backing up. The backing paint is tougher while it is soft, and the leaf cleans off most easily soon after gilding.

Frequent chipping in the backing paint is often caused by a water size that is too weak to adhere the second layer of leaf to the first during the second gild. When the two layers of leaf separate, the paint is carried away with the leaf.

Silver leaf should be used with water size for burnished gilding on glass and for no other purpose. The leaf will tarnish if gilded over varnish, either by surface gilding or with water size. Use aluminum, white gold or palladium for matte effects with burnished silver leaf outlines.

Sulphur compounds tarnish silver readily. Don't keep silver leaf where it will be subjected to industrial fumes, cooking odors, or toilet odors. Never use water containing sulphur impurities for making size; trust only distilled water. Try to avoid having silver leaf on hand for long periods.

**Plate 10.** Fire Truck. Gary Rhodes, Santa Cruz, CA. 23K lettering and scrolls, black shades, surface toning in brown with white highlights. Note detail of scroll.

**Plate 11.** Plough & Lillich. E. D. Hannaman, Newville, PA. Handcarved basswood, 2 in. thick, 23K gold leaf.

**Plate 12.** Snow Goose Inn. Susannah & Stephen Garrity, Belmont, MA. Hand-carved mahogany, 5 ft. in diameter. Lettering and scroll are gilded 23K goldfoil. Background is antiqued blue to show woodgrain texture.

Plate 13. Houlihan's. Ronn Overby, Kansas City, MO. Various karats of gold, abalone centers in "Houlihan's," color pictorial with gold accents.

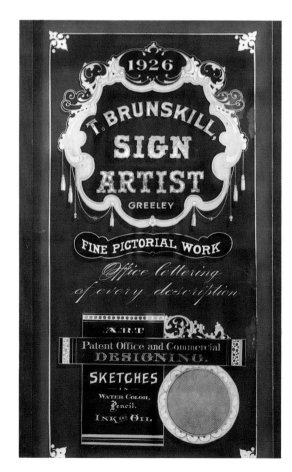

Plate 17. Zachary's. Mark Baty, Waukee, IA. Solid mahogany with 23K letters.

Plate 16. T. Brunskill. Ted Brunskill, Greeley, CO. Original 1926 shingle in various karats of gold, pearl and abalone with circle for current pictures or specialties (13½ in. x 25½ in.).

**Plate 1.** Superior Shoe Service. Kent Smith, Greeley, CO. 23K outlines, beer matte 18½ centers, 16K elongated triangles, abalone cemter "eyes," chipped borders and marble background behind pictorial of cobbler's bench.

**Plate 2.** Charles P. Rogers. Kent Smith, Greeley, CO. Company logo reproduced in gold leaf with matte and outline adaptations. Script in 23K burnished outline, 18K spun matte centers, dark Prussian blue and rose outlines. 1" copy in 23K plain gild.

**Plate 3.** Potato Brumbaugh's. Kent Smith, Greeley, CO. Sandblasted redwood, transparent red over aluminum leaf leaving aluminum outlines, "Restaurant and Saloon" 23K.

**Plate 4.** Andresen Typographics. Rick Glawson, Harbor City, CA. 20 in. high with embossed damar, various karats of gold, airbrushed pictorial and pearl.

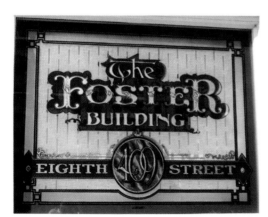

**Plate 5.** The Foster Building. Noel B. Weber, Boise, ID. Various karats of gold, glue-chipped background, abalone centers, marbled and color panels.

**Plate 6.** SIGNS of the Times October, 1984 cover. Gary Volkman, Greeley, CO. 12K masthead, 23K outlines on "Gold Leaf" with 18½K plaid center, medium green abalone centers, pearl round at bottom, magenta and lavender marble, variegated pillars. Oil color pictorial (after Alphonse Mucha).

**Plate 7.** Rhodes and Wice, P.A. W.T. Yaxley, New Port Richey, FL. 3 ft. x 13 ft. Spanish cedar, hardcarved and gilded. Detail of "830" shows brilliance of burnish.

**Plate 8.** The Optical Shop. Bob Mitchell, Escondido, CA. 23K burnished with white, pale and variegated matte, inlaid ovals of pearl, black outlines, and triple shade.

**Plate 9.** Fifth Street Grill. Mike Jackson, Moore, OK. 23K burnished outline, 23K matte with transparent lavender airbrushed on wet size, 16K burnished outline with variegated green box panel.

Plate 15. Norman Hilton. Arthur O. Sarti, Phoenix, AZ. Varieties of styles on one window.

Plate 14. Raymond H. LeBlanc's sample case. Original samples including some of the plates used to illustrate the first edition of this book.

Plate 18. Tivoli Fine Pilsner. Mark Oatis, Denver, CO. Executed in reverse on ⅜ in. plate glass, the sign employs etching, glue chipping, nine types of leaf, "mosaiced" abalone shell, "transparent" split-blended shades, airbrushing, screen printing (on center pictorial), handpainted marbling and stippled "granite" effects. The frame is wood pulp and glue-poured molding which has been gilded and antique glazed.

# 5 Surface Gilding

The term surface gilding refers to the application of leaf onto a tacky size, as described briefly in connection with gilding matte centers in glass work (Chapter 3). It is the easiest of the gilding processes. It is also used on metal or wood, individual letters of wood and plastic, trucks, and any other surface.

Tack is the sticky condition of a paint or varnish that has passed the wet stage and cannot be smeared, but is not yet dry. If the leaf is applied when the surface is still too wet, the size will come through the leaf (called *drowning the leaf*) and produce an extremely dull finish. Test the tack by touching the surface with your knuckle (Figure 89). The skin should stick slightly, but should come away clean. (Avoid using the fingertip, which will leave a print that will show through the leaf.) Another test is to run the knuckle, without pressure, over the size, which should produce a slight whistle when it is at the proper tack (hence the term *whistle tack*).

The tack of a sized surface constantly changes. It is strongest immediately after it passes from the wet stage, and this is when the leaf will adhere more readily. However, if gilding is done at a later stage, when the tack is weaker, a superior luster is obtained. Consequently the ability to judge the proper degree of tack is very useful to the gilder. Until you learn from experience how to judge the best degree of tack, a safe guide is to gild as soon as the size is dry enough so that it will not smear even when you twist your fingertip strongly against it. (This should be tried on a test area, not on a letter.)

Although it is possible to adhere gold leaf to almost any kind of paint or varnish material while it is in a tacky condition, a suitable gold size should have an exceptionally free flow (for a high-gloss finish free of brush marks) and slow surface-drying (to retain a gilding tack for a long period). Materials that dry with a surface skin pass too quickly from wet to dry and therefore do not retain the leaf well. Such materials will dry more quickly in spots where the film is thin, and it may be impossible to make the leaf adhere in these dry spots.

Suitable materials are of two types: *quick sizes*, which have a resin base and are essentially varnishes; and *slow sizes*, also called *oil sizes*, most of which have a fat linseed oil base.

**Quick Sizes**

As the name implies, materials in this group set up for gilding quite rapidly, from five minutes to three or four hours. In addition to those materials which

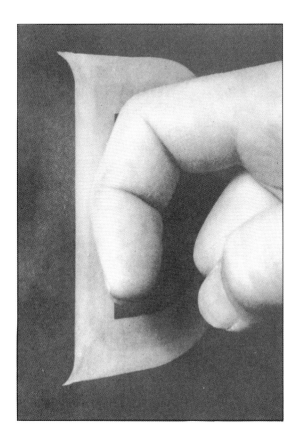

**Figure 89.** Testing the tack of gold size with a knuckle.

are sold specifically as gold sizes, this group includes the various japan varnishes and almost any kind of gloss varnish. Some paints can also be used as a quick size.

Since so many varnishes have been going off the market in the last few years, a brief description of the types is in order. Commercially produced quick size (*Chromatic Paint Corp., Commonwealth Varnish Co., Lefranc, etc.*) normally has a drying time of three to four hours. Venice japan varnish (*Commonwealth*) will gild in about an hour with a tack similar to slow size, but the tack only lasts ten minutes or so. In humid or cold weather, it tends to take longer to set up and holds a shorter tack. Florence japan varnish sets up the fastest, and will set a tack in one to one and one-half hours; it must also be gilded quickly, as its tack is short-lived.

All of these sizes do the job and making a choice is largely a matter of selecting a material whose drying time is suitable for the work to be done. On smaller jobs, a very fast-drying material is a convenience, whereas for larger jobs a slower-drying size would be a better choice to avoid having to size and gild a small section at a time. As a general rule, slower-drying sizes also take the leaf better and produce a brighter burnish.

These materials can be mixed in any combination for any length of drying time. It is possible to add quick rubbing varnish to Florence japan to produce a size that dries to tack in five minutes. This can be handy once in a while, but it is not too practical for gilding a long line of copy and has questionable durability. A word of caution: Do not use two different sizes next to each other, as they will have a different burnish and will not match each other.

Most quick sizes come in the form of uncolored liquids. For surface gilding it is necessary to mix enough color with them so that the work will show up against the background. The less color used, the better the gilding characteristics will be, which is why the sizes are produced as clears. Yellow is generally used for this purpose, since it shows up well against most other colors. Do not pick yellow in the expectation that since it is approximately the same color as gold leaf, cracks in the gild will be disguised. A crack is a crack and it will show no matter what color is underneath. On backgrounds against which yellow doesn't stand out, some dark color such as black or Prussian blue is better.

Oil colors, bulletin colors, and lettering enamels are all satisfactory for coloring the size, but japan colors have a tendency to make the size dry on the surface. Some sign painters prefer bulletin colors to tint quick size, because they take about the same time to dry.

After being worked for a while, the size gums up in the brush and on the palette and usually is applied in a thicker and slower-drying film. Therefore, the first few letters that are sized have a tendency to set up more quickly than the rest. In order to obtain an even gild, test the size with your knuckle frequently on the first few letters and gild these as soon as necessary. Don't gild too far. Do only a few letters at this time, for you will soon reach a portion that is still too wet for good gilding. After much practice and experience, you will recognize how much to palette in advance of sizing in order to produce an even tack on all the letters.

## Slow Sizes

Slow sizes have a drying period anywhere from six hours to several days. In general, slow sizes are more durable than quick sizes and for this reason are preferred for outdoor applications. Also, leaf sticks to them more easily and acquires a superior burnish. However, these three desirable qualities — durability, ease of working and good burnish cannot be obtained in the highest degree at the same time. Some principles need to be understood in this connection.

### Working Characteristics

These include three factors. (1) *The manner in which the size flows*: Slow sizes are exceptionally free-flowing, even to the point of being "runny," and so must be applied in a thin film. The runnier the brand, the thinner it must be spread. (2) *Drying time*: Slower-drying materials are less likely to dry out in spots, but the slowest-drying sizes do not usually produce the best burnishes. (3) *Retention of leaf*: Slower sizes usually retain leaf better, reducing the tendency for cracks to show in the gild; this is especially necessary when gilding work in relief, such as on wood letters or sandblasted signs.

### Burnishing Characteristics

When the size is close to being dry at the time of gilding, it will produce a higher burnish; however, it will not retain the leaf as well and is more likely to leave cracks in the gild. Better burnishes are common with the faster-drying oil sizes for the simple reason that they are likely to be more nearly dry when gilded, but slow sizes retain leaf so much better than do quick sizes that gilding can be done successfully when the tack is so slight as to seem nonexistent. Those accustomed to gilding on the stronger tack necessary with quick sizes invariably want to gild too soon on slow sizes, resulting in a dull gild. Experiment with your favorite slow size on a sample surface in the shop. Apply leaf to it on several successive days. You may find that a size that you would normally gild the next day will still take gold well after three or four days, with a higher burnish. Often a size can be left two and one-half times as long as recommended; for example, a 48-hour size might be ready in five days — and may be possible to gild even after three weeks.

**Durability**   Aside from the fact that some materials are inherently more durable than others, a thick film will be more durable than a thin one. However, the slower setting time of a thick film will decrease the amount of burnish. The nature of the surface on which size is to be applied is also a factor in how thick a size can be used. Thick films can be safely applied to flat surfaces that can be placed in a horizontal position to set. On vertical surfaces and carved work there is the danger that the size will develop runs. These dry with a surface skin that may break and produce smears when the gild is rubbed down. Only sizes that are not too runny can be applied in such work.

A considerable part of the gilder's skill lies in the ability to make good compromises between the opposing tendencies inherent in slow sizes.

It is possible to make your own fat oil size by following directions from one of the old texts, such as *Atkinson's Sign Painting* (ST Publications, 1983). It is far more convenient, however, to use commercially produced sizes, especially because they are usually more consistent from one can to the next. All of the slow sizes on the market today have their own special characteristics, which make them useful for different purposes. The most common brands currently available are made by Chromatic Paint Corp., Hastings, and Lefranc. Of these, the Lefranc size is the slowest. Depending on humidity, it takes from 18 to 30 hours to reach a good gilding tack but it has little ability to hold it for more than two days, particularly in spotty areas. When gilded over within 18 to 30 hours, Lefranc produces a good burnish. Hastings has been the most popular size for many years and still remains a consistent 18-hour size with a three-day tack. However, it does have a tendency to dry out in spots after 20 hours, but this can be avoided if the surface is completely sealed and non-absorbing. Spotty drying is more common in the company's yellow size than in the clear oil size. Hastings gives an excellent burnish and an acceptable base for ornamental burnishes. Chromatic has the same characteristics and is basically a 12- to 18-hour size, extending to 24 hours in higher humidity, but can still be gilded over in three to four days. It gives a good burnish when gilded as dry as possible and provides excellent cushion for ornamental burnishes. Hastings is the runniest of the sizes, followed by Lefranc and Chromatic in that order. Adding color sometimes makes a size less runny, and some experimentation with every new batch should be made on test pieces. Be aware that adding color will also change the consistency of the size. The best color is pictorial oil color, since it has the same base and will change the consistency the least.

All slow oil sizes can be *tempered* to change their setting times. They can be extended by adding small amounts of linseed oil or reduced by adding turpentine—or, in some rare cases, a little japan dryer. It is easier to extend the setting time, since linseed oil is compatible with the size itself. Dryers tend to make the size top-set with a wet layer underneath, causing smears when burnished. To gild a large area or a lot of individual letters, you can spray the size with a spray gun if it has been reduced by a mixture of equal amounts of linseed oil and turpentine. This will yield about a 12-hour size that will hold tack for 16 hours or longer.

Lettering enamel size is also classified as a slow size, although it has some of the characteristics of quick sizes. It can be made with Chromatic or One-Shot white or chrome yellow, diluted by about one third with slow oil size. This will produce a 4-to 6-hour size that will hold tack to a maximum of 8 hours and yield a very high luster. It can be used for ornamental burnishing if started right away. Its retention is not as good as that of a slow size, and it should be used primarily on flat or smooth surfaces. This is a handy mixture for use on truck lettering that has a lot of copy or an ornamental burnish that needs a higher burnish than possible with quick size. You should definitely test this mixture before attempting to use it on the job. You will need to become familiar with its peculiarities, since once it starts to cure past the tack stage, you have little time to gild.

Durability does not differ much between brands of slow sizes, since they are all basically of the same base. Oil-size gilding on the tombs of the ancient Egyptians and bottles produced in the Roman Empire are still intact today. Modern gilders use oil size with a virtual guarantee of permanence.

**"Burnish" Versus "Burnishing"**

A high burnish—that is, a high luster in surface gilding—is the result of having a smooth surface under the size, using a suitable sizing material, and gilding when the size is nearly dry. The last is the most important.

*Burnishing*, the term applied to the operation of rubbing down the gild with cotton- or a velvet-covered pad, is something of a misnomer. The purpose of rubbing is merely to secure the adhesion of the leaf to the size and to clean off any loose gold and wrinkles, not to add sheen. The gild actually has the highest luster before any rubbing is done. Rubbing always dulls the gild to some extent. Therefore, if the highest possible luster is desired, rub as little as possible. Use a soft brush rather than cotton or velvet. A real badger-hair shaving brush (perhaps something of an antique these days) will not scratch the gold. Other favorites are badger blenders, camel-hair water-size brushes, sable cosmetic brushes, soft fitches, and the like. Use these to lightly "dust" off the gild, removing wrinkles and covering any exposed size with gold. A brush is particularly useful for incised letters, as well as those done in relief. Gilding on carved work and round-faced, individual letters does not need the diffusing effect produced by rubbing, since on such work the surfaces are at various angles to each other and reflect light in all directions.

Bear in mind that the highest possible luster is not always the most desirable for other circumstances as well. Gilding that has a mirror-like finish will appear quite dark from certain angles, so dark, in fact, as to be unreadable, particularly on smooth surfaces. When the gild is rubbed down with cotton or velvet, it becomes covered with a network of very fine scratches that diffuse the reflected light in many directions. The gild will appear brighter from those angles with the most reflection. Since gilding that is done on wet size is dull and presents about the same appearance from any angle, it poses no reflection problems.

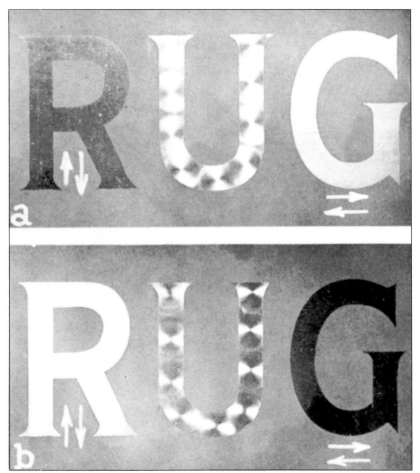

**Figure 90.** Two photographs of the same inscription illustrate the effects of the angle of illumination and the direction in which the gild was rubbed. (a) Illuminated from above. (b) Illuminated from the side. In both photographs the letter R was rubbed with vertical strokes and the letter G with horizontal strokes. Note that the spinning on the letter U is effective under both methods of illumination.

The direction of the rubbing is a matter of some importance. Ordinarily the best result is obtained by rubbing with horizontal strokes. This derives from the fact that the principal source of light is usually from above. Under these conditions, horizontal rubbing causes the reflected light to be diffused upward to some extent; a shiny surface reflects the light downward. On some indoor applications, where the leaf may be illuminated from the side, rubbing with up-and-down strokes is more effective. Figure 90 illustrates these principles and the need to consider position as well as different burnishing techniques.

During the rubbing operation, the gild should be examined from several directions. The rubbing should be continued until all parts of the gild show the same texture—and no more. You will find that it is possible to rub more extensively over a slow size, which takes the gold better and provides a better cushion.

The circular pattern produced by spinning (also called engine turning, burling, or twisting) appears bright in parts and dark in others, creating a pleasing multi-faceted effect that changes in appearance as one moves past it. It is a useful treatment for large areas, because it disguises any unevenness that may remain in the gild after rubbing. Spinning is extensively

**Figure 91.** Plaid burnished 23K with dark blue outlines, maroon shades on dark red.

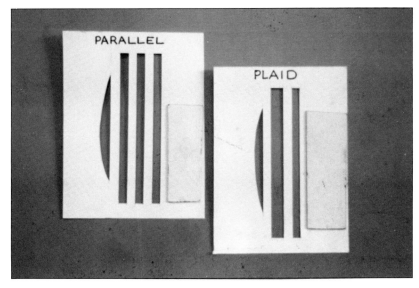

**Figure 92.** Burnishing templates, parallel for any straight line burnish and plaid template for the plaid burnish in Figure 91. See also the *SIGNS of the Times* magazine cover in the color section (Plate 6).

used on truck lettering. It is produced by turning a small pad held closely against the leaf at closely spaced intervals. (See Chapter 8, "Spinning the Leaf".)

Other patterns, such as vertical and horizontal stripes, plaids, and checkerboards, can be burnished into the gold by using a template and a cloth pad. Gary Volkman has made effective use of his grandfather's plaid burnish technique, which can be applied for other shapes as well (Figure 91). The procedure in burnishing a pattern is to make a template out of light card stock or acetate. For plaid, cut three slots: The first should be narrow; the next, wider; and the last, the same width as the first. The spaces between them should be equal to the width of the narrowest slot. A half-moon slit is cut for registration. (The template shown in Figure 92 was used to produce the plaid burnish in Figure 91.)

Holding the template at a 45° angle, burnish the open areas with a cotton or velvet pad. (A mohair roller cover works well for large areas.) Keep the alignment consistent by moving the template so that the half-moon slot is aligned over the last area burnished. To get the plaid effect, reverse the card (to the opposing angle) and burnish again right over the first burnish.

You will become aware of other patterns that can be made with similar templates, giving endless possibilities for making each gold leaf sign unique. A checkerboard pattern can be made by burnishing at right angles, leaving squares of burnished gold and squares of bright gold. Remember that this type of burnishing can be used on matte centers that have been laid on varnish size on glass.

# 6 Signboard Gilding

**Surface Preparation**

Although a slight pebble finish is not objectionable on signboards, background surfaces should generally be as smooth as possible for gilding purposes. Brush marks and other irregularities show very prominently under gold. Background paints are best sprayed or roller coated, as even enamels retain brush marks to some extent.

Some care should be taken in choosing a background paint that will cure hard and without enough tack to retain the gold applied to the letters and ornamentations. This problem can be alleviated by using lacquers and fast-drying enamels and acrylics, particularly those for automotive use. (Of course, when the background finish is to cut-in around the lettering, as on smalted signs, leaf stuck to the background will not matter.) Test the background finish prior to sizing; if the test indicates that sticking is likely, the background surface must be treated. Various preventative treatments are described in Chapter 8.

**Sizing**

As mentioned previously, slow (oil) sizes are best for outdoor signs of all types except truck lettering. They handle more easily, they yield a better burnish, and are more durable. They need no special brushes and can be lettered with gray quills, sables, or flats. Large areas can be covered with fitches and cutters. You will find it necessary to work more slowly with oil sizes than with paint or varnish sizes as oil sizes are rather thick and pull on the brush quite a bit.

Use oil sizes thick, just as they come from the can, for a more durable job. If it is desirable to thin the size, use a small amount of mineral spirits (not oleum) rather than turpentine, as turpentine dulls the finish. This effect can be avoided somewhat if a little linseed oil is added with the turpentine, but experience is necessary to keep from drastically changing the drying time. Make every effort to lay the size on evenly, and be careful not to apply too thick a film for the conditions, taking into consideration the tendency of the size to run.

When working with slow sizes, it is advisable to take measures against dust that might settle on the sized surface prior to gilding, especially if the work is not to be gilded for several days. When gilding signs in the shop, it may be convenient to leave the sign upside down and flat, either on blocks or horses. Don't turn the sign over until the size has set to the point that it won't run, or you may find a nice collection of stalactites in the size

95

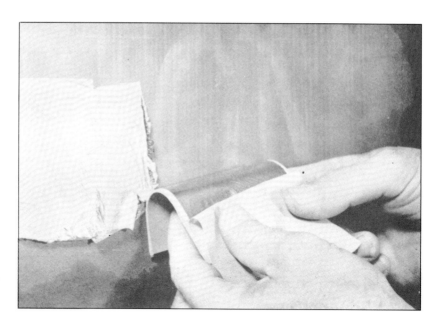

**Figure 93.** Rolling the leaf onto the surface out of the book.

the next morning. While a wet size is setting it is not time to sweep the floor, much less cut wood or spray paint nearby. A tent of plastic sheeting or plastic drop cloths can also be used to keep dust from the size, if it is sealed off well all around the upside-down sign and propped up so evaporation can take place.

**Applying the Leaf**

Using surface gold, the quickest way to gild flat work is to roll the leaf onto the sized surface directly from the book. Figure 93 explains this operation more clearly than words. You will find the work easiest when the sign surface is vertical, or nearly so, and about at waist level. In this position the book of leaf doesn't obscure your vision of the work, and it is also easier to handle.

Work in one direction only, preferably from left to right. Don't jump around. In gilding large letters it is best to lay leaf on the bottoms of the letters first and work upward, so that the weight of the hanging leaf will close the laps rather than pull them open.

Use full leaves as much as possible: There will be fewer laps to contend with, the work will go faster, and you will get a smoother job. It is actually economical to lay leaf solid on lettering up to about four inches high. When the letters are a little higher than the width of the leaf, go all the way across the bottom of the line with full leaves, then come back and gild the top portions with smaller sections. Break sections off the full leaf by rolling the book on the surface up to the edge of the size, then, sliding the book slightly, the leaf will tear at the point of contact with the background. Gild letters larger than four inches by applying sections along the letter strokes. Even on large letters you should watch for opportunities to use the full leaf, for there is no point in using two half-leaves when one full leaf will cover the same area.

Some gilders prefer to prepare strips of leaf in a convenient width. The book should be torn, not cut. Each piece of leaf is picked up together with its corresponding piece of paper for easy placement on the surface. This method of gilding is very good when static in the room makes the leaf stick to the paper.

Gold Leaf Techniques/*Signboard Gilding*

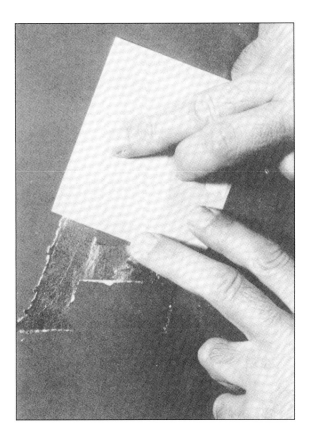

**Figure 94.** Gilding with patent leaf.

Take special care to not let the paper touch the size. Anywhere rouge gets into the size, leaf will not stick. To avoid this problem, some gilders prefer to push the leaf into the size with the hairs of a gilding tip as in glass gilding. Using the tip is somewhat slower, but has merit under many circumstances. More than likely, the job itself will dictate which method is best.

Here and there you will find small corners that can be covered with small pieces of leaf picked up with the fingers from surrounding areas, but this is not to be encouraged as a regular practice. For one thing, the amount of leaf saved is small in comparison to the time it takes. Also, if you want a good burnish, keep your fingers off the gild as much as possible. Moreover, leaf is more likely to stick to background areas that have been touched.

**Patent Leaf**   Patent leaf is sold in books of 25 standard-sized leaves, but, unlike loose gold, each leaf is lightly attached to a separate sheet of tissue paper. The paper is intended for gilding outdoors when the wind is so strong that using loose leaf would be impractical. The tissue sheet is laid on the sized surface, leaf side down and held in position with the fingers of one hand while it is rubbed with the fingers of the other hand to press the leaf into the size (Figure 94). Any leaf that doesn't come in contact with a sized area remains attached to the tissue and can be used to gild other sections. Patent leaf requires a size with a stronger tack, much like size for heavier metal leaves. Otherwise, adhesion is uncertain.

Since this method of applying patent leaf permits every scrap of gold to be utilized, some sign painters use it for all ordinary surface gilding as a means of cutting down on the cost of gold. This is foolish. They must work for a very low hourly wage in order to realize any savings by this means, because gilding with patent leaf is very slow. Others prefer to gild with patent leaf because they find using the tissue sheets "easy," but a little practice will show that gilding with surface gold directly from the book is much faster and ultimately less wasteful. Moreover, the strong pressure required to make the leaf adhere to the size encourages it to stick to the background, and the burnish does not compare to that obtainable with loose leaf. All in all, patent leaf is useful only under conditions that make it impractical to do the job with regular loose leaf.

## Roll Gold

Readers who are interested in cutting costs on large jobs may realize considerable savings by using leaf in rolls of suitable width. The area cost of roll gold is not less than book gold; the savings derive from being able to select a width of roll gold that will leave little waste. Considerable time is saved when work can be gilded with long strips, such as stripes, moldings and long lines of copy (Figure 95). Roll gold is fine for gilding individual letters, too.

Rolls are 67 feet long and are available in many different widths ranging from one-sixteenth of an inch to three inches (up to four inches on special order). The leaf is in a continuous ribbon separated by a strip of tissue paper, by which it can be handled conveniently in lengths of two feet or more.

Roll gold can be applied by hand (Figure 96) or with a gilding wheel rolled onto the surface (Figure 97). A take-up spool in the end of the wheel eliminates the mess of tissue strips that accumulate all over the floor. Gilding wheels are made in three sizes, each adjustable for rolls within a specific range of widths. A considerable amount of practice is required to use the wheel effectively, but it is well worth the effort when the job is appropriate.

## Rubbing Down the Gild

After every bit of the sized area is covered with leaf, it must be rubbed down to smooth the little wrinkles and clean off the loose gold. This can be done with cotton, a velvet pad or brush as mentioned in Chapter 5, " 'Burnish' Versus 'Burnishing '." As mentioned above, this operation is commonly called "burnishing" but has little to do with producing a high luster.

When gilding is done with quick sizes, it is usually necessary to go over the gild with a hard ball of cotton or solid velvet pad. Press the leaf into the size before attempting to rub, so that the leaf will not be torn away from the laps in the gold or the edges of quick size, where adhesion will be incomplete. Go over the entire inscription quickly and lightly to remove the majority of loose gold. Then go over the inscription again, an area at a time, with light circular strokes to catch all the wrinkles and remove the balance of the loose gold. Your brush or pad can be cleaned into a skewings box to reclaim the gold or to merely dispose of the excess.

If the job needs either the highest possible luster or a spun finish, stop rubbing at this point. Otherwise, continue rubbing to bring the gild to the proper diffused texture for the location and light (page 92).

Once more, if for any reason gilding has been done on fairly wet size, any rubbing must be done very lightly so as not to drown the leaf.

**Figure 95.** Gilding a half-round moulding with roll gold.

**Figure 96.** Gilding with roll gold by hand.

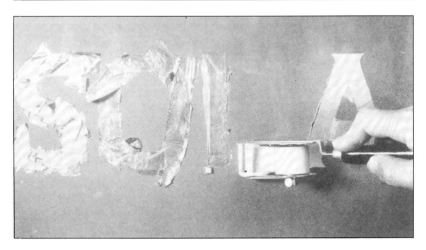

**Figure 97.** Gilding with roll gold and a gilding wheel.

### Carved and Sandblasted Wood Signs

Across the country, signs are being made of various woods, using various techniques to incise either the artwork or the background. Sandblasting heads the list, followed by hand-carving and routing. Although redwood has been the most popular wood, sugar pine, mahogany, walnut, oak, basswood, and maple have all been used. However, the technique for gilding all of these is fairly universal and much the same as for other surfaces, with a few enhancements to make the work easier.

Letters that are sandblasted in relief are among the easiest to gild. If pre-primed before blasting, they can be sized without further preparation. Any left-over adhesive from the sandblasting mask must be removed, of course, as the size will not stick over it. Gilding looks best on only the surface of the inscription, and care must be taken to select a size that will not run down the edges of the relief (usually a slow oil size). Make the selection based on the same considerations affecting other surface gilding. Gild in the usual manner for surface gold and rub with a soft brush. Any loose gold that gets down into the background can be removed with a vacuum.

If you stain or paint the background before removing the sandblasting mask and gilding, be certain that it is thoroughly dry, or the gold will stick. Some sign painters have found that water-based latexes and acrylics will work best, since these paints have no tack and dry rapidly; others question their durability. Commercial, light oil stains also cure rapidly, although they tend to form puddles that do not dry easily. You should be aware of the type of finish that will have the best durability in the climate of your area. You may need to conduct your own tests. Incised, sandblasted letters can be gilded under some circumstances. The determining factor is the type of wood and its grain pattern. The veins will cause the gold to skip in areas, leaving a dull raw wood line in the gild. This is found in all vertical grain patterns, but is frequently found in others as well.

Gilding on incised, hand-carved letters requires a smooth surface and is difficult on letters that are not well executed. The raw wood of the letter must be primed either with two or three coats of size or a coat of primer or burnishing sealer. Care must be taken to avoid puddles of size in the crevices, or wet spots of size may be rubbed up and spoil the gild. Gild by laying on sheets of surface gold (many prefer to use a gilders tip), and then push the leaf into the incised letter with a soft brush such as a badger shaving brush, soft fitch, or the like. For a brilliant burnish apply the leaf when the tack is barely perceptible; since you are already using the soft brush, no rubbing is necessary. Backgrounds that are to be stained or painted must be finished before gilding, with the same precautions on drying as noted above.

Incised, routed letters are gilded in the same way, although you may find that the bottoms of the letters may need to be smoothed out with sandpaper or a hand-carving chisel. The same is true of routed letters left in relief, as the edges are rarely clean and require sanding and finishing.

These methods are much the same as those used to gild letters incised in stone (see Chapter 9).

**Matching Old Work**

Occasionally a job will come in that calls for adding or changing a line on an old gilded sign or on an office door. Gilding that has been in service for some time acquires a *patina*, which tones down the sheen and gives a deeper color than freshly laid gold leaf. Here you can take advantage of the dulling effect of gilding on wet size and possibly rub a little more than normal. Wiping over the fresh gild with damp cotton immediately after gilding also tones down the "new" look and brings the color closer to that of the old work.

If the original varnish has darkened, its color can be approximated by tinting the varnish for the new portion with a very little raw umber or burnt umber oil color as needed.

**Smalt Backgrounds**

Smalt can be either sea sand or finely-broken, ground, colored glass. Either type can be sprinkled on top of wet paint or varnish to produce the smooth, velvety surface always admired as a background for gold leaf. Obviously, sand smalt is less expensive than glass. It is usually finer and clings to the adhering paint better than the coarser glass smalt. Sand smalt also has a duller appearance, which is often preferred. Most sand smalts available today are black, but some ingenuity will give you any color desired. Clean beach sand can be colored by adding japan color mixed with quick rubbing varnish and thinned with mineral spirits to stain consistency. Stir the sand and paint mixture constantly until all the sand is stained, then dry it by tossing it through an inclined screen. It will probably have to be sifted in this manner a number of times to keep it from sticking together, but this turn-of-the-century method was common everywhere and still works well. If you can't get beach sand, try sands sold for sandblasting, mortar, or children's play.

By their nature, glass smalts produce a shinier finish that sparkles in the sunlight and attracts more attention, even in indoor applications. The fact that the color is permanent is an important advantage. Some gilders prefer a mixture of sand and glass, although it is difficult to get an even mixture.

The white lead formerly used to adhere the smalt is no longer available. Use titanium white oil paste such as Chromatic Pictorial Oil Color or titanium/zinc paste white from One-Shot as a substitute. The mixture is the same as noted in many old texts. Add enough black oil paste (ivory black is preferable) to the white to make a dark gray. To this mixture add one-fourth varnish for adhesion and drier with enough raw linseed oil to increase flow and extend drying time. The paint should stay wet enough to allow dusting the smalt onto wet paint for best adhesion. Cut in around the letters or inscription with the mixture as heavy as can be brushed.

Smalt should be sifted onto the paint while it is still wet. The simplest sifter can be made by merely punching or drilling holes all over the bottom of a large, two- or three-pound coffee can. The holes should be about one-eighth of an inch in diameter so that the smalt will run through freely. A slightly more elaborate sifter can be made by cutting both ends of the can, then fastening a wire screen over one end. Place the can on a square of heavy cardboard while you fill it with smalt, then lift the can and cardboard together and carry them over to the sign, which should be laid flat on the floor on top of a clean drop cloth. Take the cardboard away from the bottom of the can to let the smalt run onto the sign. Hold the smalt can fairly close to the sign to avoid scratching the gold as the sand falls.

Sift on the smalt in a good layer, about one-fourth of an inch thick (Figure 98). The excess that doesn't cling to the paint can be dumped off onto the drop cloth and returned to the container for future use by turning the sign upside down quickly. If the sign is turned over too slowly, a good deal of smalt will be dislodged from the paint by the loose smalt sliding over the surface. Adhesion will be better if the loose smalt is left on the sign overnight and not disturbed until the paint has set. This is the preferred method if your shop has adequate space.

When a background is so large or so complicated that it cannot be painted completely with the smalt paint in an hour or two, it can be painted and smalted in sections. When sifting smalt onto one section, don't go all

**Figure 98.** Sifting on the smalt using a coffee can with ⅛ inch holes drilled all over the bottom.

**Figure 99.** A narrow black paint outline is used to achieve a clean edge on smalt work.

the way to the edge of the paint. Leave a few inches unsmalted in order to make a smooth lap with the next section. When painting and smalting in sections this way, a new section should be started about once every half hour so that there won't be a big difference in the set of the paint where one section joins another.

After dumping off the loose smalt, you will usually find that a few grains still cling here and there on the gilding and the painted borders. They will need to be cleaned off with a dust brush, but not before the smalt paint has had a chance to dry. If the schedule will permit, it is wise to keep the sign in the shop for a week after applying the smalt, for anything that rubs against a smalted background before the paint is cured will leave a mark that is impossible to repair.

When lettering is cut-in with smalt paint, the grains of smalt will make the edges somewhat ragged. This is not objectionable on large work, but, when the lettering is small (three inches or less), a much neater job can be done by adding a narrow outline of black between the edges of the letter and the smalted background. The paint for this outlining is best if it has a flat or satin finish. Outline the letter first, then cut in the smalt paint to the edge of the outline or to within one-sixteenth of an inch of the edges of the letters (Figure 99). It is not necessary to be fussy about the width of the outline or to finish the corners, since the smalt paint will cover irregularities. The black outline must be dry before the smalting operation is done, or the smalt will stick to it and defeat its purpose.

# 7 Dimensional Letters

Most any cut-out, individual letter can be gilded. Wood letters have been the most common over the years and are covered in detail in the next sections. Metal letters need only be primed with a good metal primer, such as an oxide or an automotive primer, before they can be sized and gilded in the same manner as wood letters.

Plastic letters can also be gilded. But why gild cheap plastics? Since some plastics are relatively permanent, their durability makes them a good choice for many situations. They are also available in many letter styles and can be easily enhanced by gold. They are easily prepared for gilding simply by roughening the surface slightly with a lacquer thinner or fine sandpaper to give it a tooth for the size to stick to. The letters are then sized and gilded in the same process as wood letters. Choose a light-colored letter to best camouflage imperfections or scratches in heavy metal leaves.

**Wood Letters**     Gilded wood letters have experienced a rebirth in popularity, particularly in pedestrian malls, interior mall and store applications, as well as restoration areas. They have an "expensive" look and, when properly constructed and properly finished, they last a long time. It is not unusual to see good-looking gilded wood letters that have been in service for 30 to 40 years (Figure 100). Many readers will know of a nearby Woolworth store whose gilded wood letters are still intact.

Commercially available wood letters are produced in several cross-sectional shapes, but for gilding purposes the half-round style (sometimes called two-thirds round) is usually preferred. In this style, a portion of the edge near the back of the letter is cut straight and can be painted with the background color or with some contrasting color. Only the rounded face is gilded. On letters cut with flat surfaces, the faces are usually the only portions gilded; the returns are painted to enhance the relief effect of the letters.

While it may seem feasible to cut and finish wood letters yourself, ordering pre-manufactured letters is considerably more profitable unless you have a complete wood shop and an order large enough to warrant the time required to produce them. A look through the catalogs will show how inexpensive it can be to purchase rather than make letters yourself. Spanjer Bros., Inc., Chicago, has been producing stock wood letters for nearly 100 years and is able to match older letter styles.

**Figure 100.** Gilded wood letter sign.

## Construction Details

Sign faces supporting wood or other cut-out letters must be constructed in such a manner that they will last as well and look as nice as the letters themselves. The most common material is framed sheet metal. Any metal used must be of a sufficiently heavy gauge to avoid warping, which can break wood letters in time. A 24- or 22-gauge, electroplated sheet (*Paint-Lok, Paint-Grip*, or the like) works well. The framing can be lumber or steel, depending on your capabilities. Be sure to make provision for lifting, since larger signs will require installation by a sign crane or similar procedure.

Automotive finishes can be used successfully on the sign face, since they adhere well to metal, are flexible, and have excellent color retention. When spray-painted, the finish is superlative and gives a slick, clean backdrop for the gold letters.

Attach wood letters from the back with screws. Sheet metal screws hold in wood better than conventional wood screws, and, since they have less taper and sharper threads, they are less likely to split the wood. They should be long enough to go about halfway through the letters. It is imperative that holes be drilled in the backs of the letters to receive the screws. Omitting this detail is very bad practice and is sure to result in the letter's splitting—perhaps not immediately, but after the sign has been up for a while. The holes in the letters should be drilled as large as the solid part of the screw at the bottom of the threads, never smaller.

Locating the holes in the sign face and in the letters so that they will register calls for a little engineering. After the letters have been sanded to finished size, but before they have been painted, lay them out on the sign in correct position and trace around them to mark the background (Figure 101). Remove the letters and drill the fastening holes in the sign face, inside the letter outlines (Figure 102). Drill these holes somewhat larger than the body of the screws to permit some slight lateral adjustment in case the holes in the letters don't line up exactly. Then hold the letters in position, one at a time, and mark the location for the holes on the backs of the letters.

105

**Figure 101.** Tracing around letter with chalk prior to gilding.

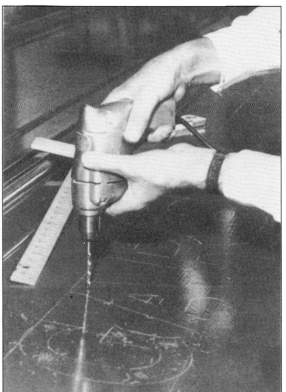

**Figure 102.** Drilling holes in sign background for fastening letters.

**Figure 103.** Brads driven into the holes serve as legs for the letters to rest on while they are being painted.

The best way to do this is to use the same drill that was used for the sign face to drill slightly into the wood from the back of the sign. Don't drill full-sized holes in the letters at this time; instead drive one and one-half inch brads into the hole locations to serve as legs for the letters to rest on while they are being painted (Figure 103).

The letters can be prepared for mounting on walls and other backgrounds by pre-drilling and inserting nails, screws (then cutting the heads off), or all-thread for use as mounting studs. Make a paper pattern of the letters, then mark the location of these studs on the paper for use as a drill pattern. Simply tape up the pattern and drill through it at the points marked and the letters will be in perfect position. This type of mount is used extensively inside stores and malls when the letters look best mounted on the wall itself. A small amount of panel adhesive or silicone will hold the letter in place.

From this point on, it is necessary to keep the letters in order to avoid transposing two of the same letter. Mark the back side of the letter with a number or some other method to identify them. The tops of O's, I's, N's and Z's should be marked; if these letters are turned around, the holes won't match. Bear in mind that periods are normally smaller than dots over i's and j's, and mark them so that they won't be switched.

## Sanding

It is possible to size and gild wood letters after merely applying two or three coats of paint on them just as they come from the factory, but quality work isn't done this way. Wood letters are normally shipped with many surface irregularities, and, unless these are sanded off, they will show up prominently under gold. Since sanding wood in the beginning is much easier than sanding paint, particularly on letters, spend the time to sand first rather than waste time sanding later.

Before doing any sanding, go over the surface of the letters, front and back, with a soaking wet sponge, wetting the wood thoroughly enough to "raise the grain." Let them dry overnight. The principle behind this is

107

**Figure 104.** Sanding the faces of wood letters. A light placed low and to the side shows up any surface irregularities.

not generally understood, and is explained by the fact that soft wood is compressed to some extent when worked with wood tools. The softer parts of the grain are compressed more than the hard portions. This compressed wood tries to regain its original shape and, given enough time, will do so. As a consequence, the soft parts will eventually be raised higher than the rest, and the surface will become irregular. Wetting the wood accelerates the process, so that the high spots can be sanded off and the surface will then stay true. Unless this is done, the grain will be raised by the paint that is applied, and it will then be too late to smooth the surface without cutting through to the bare wood.

Sand with a good-quality, aluminum oxide or carborundum paper. Start with a coarse grade, using light pressure to cut off only the high spots without making deep scratches in the wood. Some finishing may be necessary with very fine paper or a *Scotchbrite* pad. The best way to see your progress is to work in a dark area with a single strong light placed to one side and at nearly the same level as the bench. This will show up every irregularity of the surface (Figure 104). Remember that the gold will make any imperfections even more prominent. It will take quite a bit of sanding before the surface is true. Round off the back edge to make the letters easier to prime (Figure 105).

Make sure to do a thorough job of cleaning off the sanding dust before applying the priming coat, or you will have a rough surface. A shop vacuum (Figure 106) does the best job. Clean the shop area as well before priming so that no dust will settle in the primer, much less the gold size.

**Priming**  The manner in which bare wood is primed will, to a great extent, determine the durability of the painted sign when exposed to the weather. Therefore,

**Figure 105.** The sanding job is completed by rounding off this edge, which makes it much easier to paint the letters.

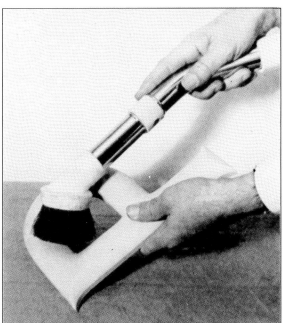

**Figure 106.** Clean off the sanding dust with a vacuum cleaner.

it is important to understand the theories behind wood finishing.

When bare wood is exposed to the weather, the outside portions of the wood absorb moisture readily during wet periods, and the wood swells. When the weather becomes dry, the surface wood gives up its moisture and shrinks. However, water penetrates into the deeper portions of wood slowly, and these interior portions are relatively unaffected by normal weather changes. This gives rise to a continuous back-and-forth strain between the surface wood and the deeper layers and ultimately causes checking and warping. Paints and other materials are applied on wood to prevent this action.

Sealing the surface of the wood to prevent the absorption of moisture is a fallacy. Surface finishing of wood never completely prevents the entrance of moisture, and, if that were our aim in painting wood, we should have to admit failure. However, a film of paint does greatly slow down the free movement of water into and out of the wood, so that the moisture diffuses evenly throughout the entire piece, eliminating surface checking. Latex and acrylic paints, as well as others designed to cover wood with a "protective" coating, do not fill the sign painter's needs for preserving wood.

For durability, a surface coating must be flexible enough to resist the normal expansion and contraction of the wood. The first coat applied must have the ability to cling strongly to the wood, and each subsequent coat must bond firmly to the layer underneath if the entire film is to remain intact.

When a pigment/vehicle mixture of any kind is applied to bare wood, most of the vehicle soaks into the wood, whereas most of the pigment stays on the surface, with little vehicle to bind it together. This is because the openings in wood are much too tiny to allow particles of pigment to pass through, except in the end grain. When a second coat of paint is applied, the dry pigment of the first coat will soak up and rob oil from the second coat, which in turn will take oil from the third coat, resulting in a weak paint film throughout.

The best sort of primer to use on bare wood is therefore a liquid containing no pigment. It must also dry sufficiently to act as a sealer against penetration of oil from subsequent coats. Finally, it must remain flexible for a long time and provide a good bond with subsequent coats of paints.

One such material is linseed oil, and it has been recommended as a primer by many in the business. Wood treated properly with linseed oil will give excellent service. However, linseed oil requires a long drying period before the first coat of paint can safely be applied, at least a week if boiled oil is used and much longer for raw oil. If paint is applied before the linseed oil primer is dry, it may penetrate the wood, take an extended time to dry, and also wrinkle and crack. An indication that the primer is not sealing effectively is that the coat of paint applied on top of it dries with dull spots.

Some of the newer, synthetic liquid primers, such as X-I-M *Flash Bond* or *Chromatic Wood Primer*, provide satisfactory sealing in a much shorter drying time. Two coats of these materials should be applied on wood letters to seal the heavy proportion of end grain (Figure 107). Allow the first coat to dry overnight, for although these primers dry very fast when applied to wood without end grain, any solvents that penetrate into the grain evaporate only after a considerable amount of time. The second coat should be given six hours or so to dry before the first coat of paint is applied. These primers replace the old-timer's method of triple coating with white lead and linseed oil and covering knots with shellac.

Follow priming with two coats of bulletin color, or better yet, with a lettering enamel such as One-Shot or Chromatic. It is a good plan to tint each coat a different color as a control against leaving holidays. Apply the

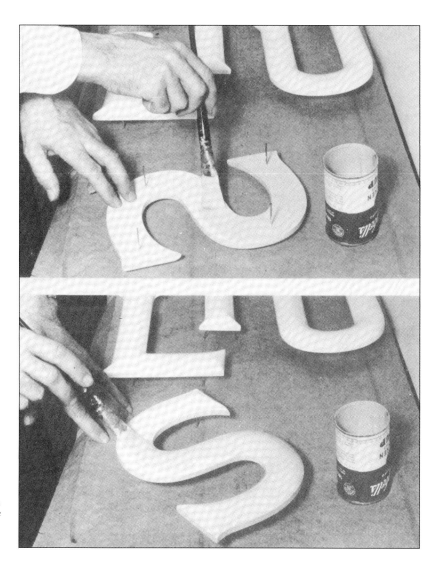

**Figure 107.** Painting the letters. Backs are painted first, then the letters rest on the brads while the faces are painted. Each coat is tinted a different color as a control against leaving holidays.

paint liberally with a spray gun or a soft brush so as to obtain a surface free of brush marks. For long life, the backs of wood letters should be painted with as many coats as the faces. Paint the backs first, then rest them on their brads to paint the faces. Give the letters a final sanding with Scotchbrite or 200-grit paper before applying gold size.

**Fastening Letters to the Sign**

To keep from cracking the wood letter, pre-drill the fastening holes (Figure 108). Using a stop on the drill will prevent the drill from going too deep. Attach the letters with sheet-metal screws through the background.

On signs with a smalted background, it is customary to size and gild the letters in place on the sign before smalting the background. In this way we avoid having to handle the letters when they are freshly gilded, when the gild is quite delicate. The smalt paint is cut in around the letters and extended up onto the straight portion of the edges (Figure 109).

Signs with painted backgrounds (not smalt) can be done in the same manner. However, it is better on such jobs to finish the background

111

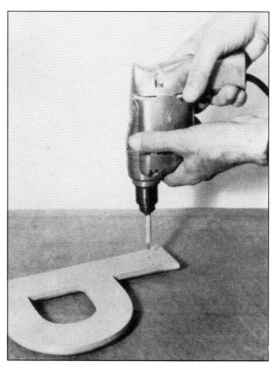

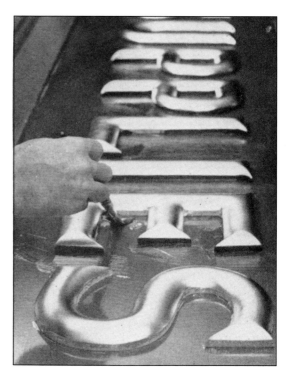

**Figure 108.** Drilling holes in the backs of the letters for the attaching screws. Note the stop on the drill to prevent it from going too deep.

**Figure 109.** Cutting in with smalt paint. The smalt paint is brought up onto the straight portion of the letters, as shown.

and the letters separately before the letters are attached. This makes it possible to paint the edges of the letters in a contrasting color. The edges of gold letters for a sign with a white background might be painted black or some other color, for instance. This procedure makes it unnecessary to cut in the background paint around the letters.

On jobs done in this manner, the letters will last longer if they are studded out from the background, even as little as a quarter of an inch. This provides air space so that water cannot remain behind the letters after a rain or freeze. The mechanics are simple. A sleeve of proper length is slipped over the fastening screws between the letter and the background. Sections cut from plastic tubing are ideal for this purpose. They can be made any desired length and are noncorrosive. For only a slight extension, two plastic washers or similar pieces can be used.

## Gilding

Wood letters are generally sized with a good, slow oil size (Figure 110). It is advisable to brush the size out thin, because wood letters have many crevices where the size can collect into pools. The letter surfaces, brushes, and the size must all be clean, because every little speck of lint or dust will be magnified ten times on the gilded surface. They, too, make the size collect in droplets that might still be liquid at the time of gilding and smear during the rubbing operation. Foreign particles should be picked off the surface with a corner of the brush.

Brushing the size is preferable to spraying, as you can control the evenness of the coat. On larger jobs, it may only be practical to spray, reducing the size with a linseed/turpentine mixture.

Don't gild too soon. Allow two to three times the recommended drying time in order to obtain a good burnish. Follow the guidelines mentioned

**Figure 110.** Sizing the letters.

under Chapter 5, "Slow Sizes." In cold weather, even more time than this must be allowed if the shop is heated only during working hours. Don't gild while the sized surface is cold, as there won't be enough tack to take the gold. The tack will come back when it gets warm again.

Leaf can be applied directly from the book (Figure 111) or in torn strips. Roll gold can also be used advantageously (Figure 112), although it must be applied manually rather than by wheel.

One of the easiest methods of gilding wood letters is to apply the leaf with the gilding tip, particularly for those familiar with glass gilding. If a tip is used, the leaf can be cut with the fingernail into sections of just the proper width and then positioned accurately on the letters as in glass gilding. This eliminates a lot of wasted gold. The use of the tip also makes it easy to wrap the leaf over the rounded faces of the letters (Figure 113). Last, but not least, gilding with the tip keeps the fingers off the letters, and this is an important contribution toward getting a good burnish.

A soft brush, such as a water-size or badger-hair brush, is handy to push the leaf into the corners as you gild. The brush can also be stroked through the hair, like a gilding tip, to pick up small pieces of leaf. A soft brush (such as a water-size or badger-hair shaving brush) is also the best tool for cleaning off loose gold.

The temptation will be strong to patch holidays with skewings. However, a much brighter and more satisfactory gild will result if fresh leaf is used for patching. Because the skewings are always somewhat crumpled

113

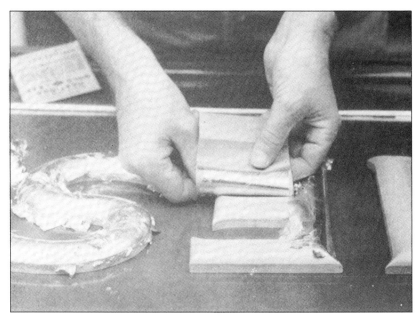

**Figure 111.** Gilding letters directly from the book.

**Figure 112.** Gilding letters with roll gold. Handle the roll as shown. A gilding wheel is not practical for work on curved surfaces.

and have been handled with the fingers, they are not conducive to a good burnish and result in a dull gild.

After all the bare spots have been filled with leaf, the final rubdown can be done with cotton, velvet or a brush (Figures 114 and 115). This is done with a random circular motion, using just enough pressure to wipe off the wrinkles. Stubborn wrinkles are best smoothed out by rubbing them lengthwise. You will discover that quite a bit of rubbing will be required before every wrinkle is smoothed down, but, to retain as much luster in the gild as possible, don't rub any longer or any harder than necessary.

Wood letters gilded with slow size need no protective coating. The

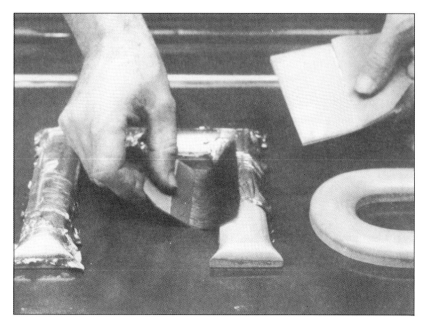

**Figure 113.** Gilding letters with the glass gilding tip.

**Figure 114.** Brushing off loose gold with a water-size brush.

gilded surface will withstand the elements better than any varnish or man-made coating that might be applied, and varnish applied on top of highly burnished gold dulls the luster to some extent.

**Renovating Gilded Letters**

The gilding on old wood letters can often be brightened up considerably simply by washing, as their dullness is often merely the result of dirt. Use mild soap and water, not detergents or abrasive cleaners. A vinegar solution will remove some other stains. If this treatment does not brighten the gild sufficiently, the best thing to do is to regild. Lightly sand the letters or use Scotchbrite to ensure good adhesion of the size, and gild as with new letters. Of course, if the paint is peeling, spot-prime the affected areas.

**Figure 115.** Final smoothing of the gild with cotton.

Smalted backgrounds that have faded or worn thin can be restored by painting right over the old smalt and re-smalting, provided that the paint isn't peeling from the sign surface. The surface will be a little rougher than the original, but it is usually satisfactory. Be sure to lay on a good thick film of smalt paint on this type of restoration.

# 8 Truck Gilding

Many trucks on the streets have painted lettering that should have been done in gold. In fact, many of these would be gold leaf jobs if the sign painter had used a little imagination and sold *gold leaf signs* rather than *gold leaf*.

Many sign painters will say, "Gold is too expensive and I can't sell it." If the truth were known, these people are most likely afraid of the gold leaf process and consequently are pricing it out of the reach of the average customer. A gilder who knows materials and is familiar with handling gold leaf can letter a truck in gold in the same time that it takes to do a good, two-coat paint job. The gold size used on trucks is as easy to work with as any lettering paint and actually can be lettered faster than enamels by those with good brush technique. It should not take any longer to gild the lettering than it does to paint the second coat so often required by popular color combinations. The additional cost of a gold job therefore represents only the cost of the leaf (two or three books, on the average) plus the time to varnish over the lettering, which together shouldn't increase the price as much as fifty percent. Anyone who can't sell gold on this basis is a poor salesman. Remember that not all of the lettering on a truck need be gold to be effective. Sometimes only a portion of the copy lends itself to being gilded while the rest is better if painted, instead. These applications can be real eye-catchers and turn identification on a truck into advertising on a truck. A consideration for quality, non-fading durability and the custom look of gold is always acceptable to the customer.

## Surface Preparation

The surface of a truck should be clean before starting any lettering, whether gold or paint. The body may have a coating of wax or polish, sometimes without the knowledge of the truck owner. There may be a film of oil deposit from exhaust fumes that will cause leaf to stick to the surface and may prevent paint from bonding properly. The same is true of airborne particles and pollution. Silicone-based automotive finishes must also be treated to remove silicone that may have risen to the surface.

The first step of good cleaning is to use a silicone and wax solvent on the surface. *DuPont 3812S Reducer, DuPont Prep-Sol,* and *111 Trichoroethane* are excellent for this purpose. Wipe the surface with a dampened, clean cloth and dry with as many dry cloths or paper towels as necessary to keep from spreading any residue onto the area. Once the surface is dry, clean again with Bon Ami, just as you would a window. Work up a good

117

lather with a wet rag or sponge, allow it to dry on the surface, and then wipe it clean with dry rags or cotton. *Important*: Should you find it difficult to wipe off the dry Bon Ami powder cleanly, there is still wax on the surface. In such cases, repeat the application of Bon Ami, two or three times if necessary, until the dry powder wipes off easily. Only at this point is it safe to apply paint.

Another indication that the clean surface is ready for lettering is a trace of the body color on the wiping rag, which means that the Bon Ami is biting into the surface. This is not to say that you should damage the surface, but this slight scratching will allow the paint to adhere, yet not be noticed.

Before putting the layout on a truck, test to see if the leaf will stick to the finish. Lay a piece of leaf on the surface, press it hard with the ball of the thumb, and then wipe it off clean with dry cotton. If it sticks slightly, but can be wiped off easily with damp cotton, it is probably safe to proceed. To be on the safe side, repeat the test on other portions of the truck. Usually there will be no sticking problem on original factory finishes after they are cleaned with Bon Ami. Bad cases of sticking are more likely to be encountered on repainted bodies, especially when you get them fresh from the paint shop, as is usually the case.

Sticking is also more prevalent in humid weather. The leaf may even begin to stick part way through the job if the humidity level of your working environment changes, such as might be the case if you are working in a garage when other trucks are brought in for a wash.

When the test shows that sticking can be expected, there are various preventative treatments. The simplest is to pounce the surface lightly with talcum or whiting, but this is not the most effective. A better method is to rub the surface with a cut raw potato, which will leave a coating of starch on the surface. Each of these methods creates problems during the gilding operation, however. A powdery deposit is apt to be picked up on the leaf and will prevent the leaf from adhering to the size. This is especially likely when applying leaf directly from the book and sliding it on the surface to break off a section. Also, the powder may be carried into holidays when the gild is rubbed, making these places difficult to patch. For these reasons, egg size is a better preventative against sticking.

Egg size (which is *not* used for applying the gold) is prepared by mixing the white of one egg in a half-pint of cold water. Part vinegar can be used in place of half of the water if this size does not adhere to the surface well enough. The mixture is then strained through a fine-mesh cloth. Much of the egg white will be retained in the cloth, but enough will be in the solution to do the job. Use a water-size brush to flow the prepared size liberally over the surface to be lettered, and allow it to dry before lettering. Apply two coats for particularly bad cases of sticking, when the truck finish is noticeably tacky. Egg size has been used successfully on surfaces that were so tacky that they took gold leaf as readily as the gold size itself. Under very humid conditions, the egg size itself may become so tacky that leaf may stick to it, but will wipe right off with damp cotton or chamois.

Simple layouts can be worked out with chalk or Stabilo right on the truck surface, but it is always better to make pounce patterns, especially since the lettering will be repeated on the other side of the truck. When the truck is to be lettered away from the shop, it is often more convenient to make patterns on the job rather than to make an extra trip for measurements. Carry a roll of paper and a perforating board for this purpose. If you are familiar with the model, however, you may be able to make the pattern in advance. It is always easier to draw a better pattern and to perforate it cleaner on the shop bench (particularly with an electric perforator). You can better visualize the layout if you tape the paper on the truck and rough-out the pattern before cleaning it up on the bench.

Unless the inscription is intricate, it is not necessary to draw the pattern in complete detail. Usually top and bottom guidelines and a rough indication of the letter spacing will suffice. If your lettering ability is not solid enough to work from a single-line pattern, gold leaf work will be laborious and difficult.

## The Silicone Problem

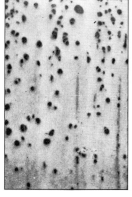

**Figure 116.** "Fish-eyes" caused by silicone under the gold size. Shown at actual size.

Fortunately you can detect the presence of silicone on a surface right after it is sized. Silicone gives rise to a peculiar type of crawling, little crater-like depressions in the paint known as fish eyes (Figure 116). The amazing thing about these fish eyes is that the paint or varnish film isn't completely broken, but is merely thinner inside the craters. Sign painters are tempted to ignore this condition and go right on sizing and gilding, for it is still possible to obtain an unbroken gild right over the fish eyes. But beware—you can confidently expect the gold to peel, since the fish eye has little size to hold the gild and is contaminated with silicone, which is well-known as an anti-sticking agent.

When fish eyes are encountered and additional cleaning with Prep-Sol or 3812S does not cure the problem, then another step must be considered. A material known as fish-eye eliminator can be obtained from auto paint dealers. One well-known brand available is *Smoothie*. Fish-eye eliminator is simply silicone liquid, and adding a drop or two to your size or paint will give it a silicone base. Although it does tend to increase the adhesion, it is not intended as a bonding agent; it merely combines with the silicone on the surface to allow the paint or size to flow freely. Any subsequent coats of size or paint must now also be treated in order to stick. (Chromatic Overcoat Clear varnish is already treated.)

Great care must be taken that any silicone compounds are not allowed to contaminate other paints, brushes, paint rags, or brush rinse. Brushes should be very thoroughly cleaned in solvent, which should then be discarded along with the rags.

## Gold Size

The choice of size can be an important factor in making truck lettering go smoothly. Quick sizes are generally used, but require that you gild only small sections and constantly check the tack. Synthetic quick size is handy for jobs with little copy and takes less time to set up.

Lettering enamel tempered with slow size works particularly well. Mix three parts of One-Shot or Chromatic lettering enamel with one part slow oil size for a four- to six-hour set-up time. Extend the time by adding extra oil size; decrease the oil size for a size that will set up in about two hours. Color the size for good visibility against the particular background.

Some sign painters prefer to use slow size for lettering trucks. Gilding is a little easier on a slow size and obtains a better burnish. This is ideal if you can have the truck in your shop under controlled conditions for a few days. On large jobs, such as fire trucks, there is the added advantage that all

**Figure 117.** Spinning the gold. Here a foam rubber pad covered with velvet has been mounted on a spindle and used in an electric drill to create an extremely brilliant effect. Use of the drill also makes the work go much faster.

the sizing can be done at one time and the gilding can be done all in one operation on another day. However, for the average truck-lettering job, which needs to be completed (except for varnishing) in one day there isn't much point in using slow size and spreading the work over a longer period of time.

**Gilding**

The actual gilding should present no problems if the basic principles are followed. If powder is used as a precaution against sticking and is carried into holidays so that they are difficult to patch, you may succeed in getting leaf to stick in these places by moistening the spot with damp cotton or by wetting a fingertip with saliva and applying leaf while the spot is still damp. If holidays are numerous, it is an indication that you are gilding when the size is too dry or that the size you are using isn't suitable. Gilding trucks should be done as soon as the size becomes too dry to smear and still has a strong tack. A high burnish isn't obtained this way, but on truck lettering a high burnish isn't too important.

Occasionally, and in spite of every precaution, leaf may still stick to the background. This is always aggravating. When sticking occurs, try the following remedies, in the order listed: (1) Wipe with damp cotton. (2) Wash with damp cotton and mild soap; this is usually effective, and the gild won't be harmed if it is done gently. (3) In really stubborn cases, complete the job without removing the stuck leaf. If the lettering is to be varnished, apply varnish accurately just to the edges of the letters in those areas where gold is stuck on the background. Wait a few days until the varnish is good and dry, and then rub off the blemishes with automobile rubbing or polishing compound. (4) Sometimes it is practical to cut-in a panel around the lettering, which of course will do away with the bad spots. (5) A pencil eraser can be used to remove small stubborn spots here and there, but it is not practical for large areas.

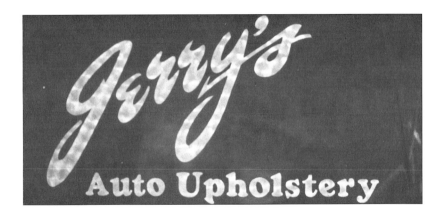

**Figure 118.** A spun gold inscription on a mini-van.

**Spinning the Leaf**

Also called engine turning, twisting or burling, spinning the leaf is a simple operation and greatly enhances the appearance of truck lettering. It becomes especially effective when the lettering is varnished.

The simplest way to do this is to make a small ball of cotton, press it moderately hard against the gilded surface with the fingers and give it a half twist. This is repeated along the letter strokes at closely spaced intervals, touching each other but preferably not overlapping.

A better tool can be made by covering the cotton with velvet. Because it produces finer and more even scoring, velvet's effect will also be more brilliant. Such a pad can be mounted on a spindle and used in an electric drill, preferably one with variable speed in order to be able to work slowly enough to control the pattern (Figure 117). The pad pictured was made by gluing foam rubber three quarters of an inch thick onto a large spool cut in half and fitted with a long, quarter-inch stove bolt to go into the drill chuck. The velvet cover is renewed often, as soon as it begins to lose its nap.

The spinning must be done immediately after gilding, before the size has a chance to dry. Plaid or other styles can also be done as detailed in Chapter 5, " 'Burnish' Versus 'Burnishing'."

**Ornamentation**

Gold truck lettering is seldom left plain. It is usually ornamented—more or less elaborately—with outlines, shades, highlights, centers, or other effects. Outlining is the most common and the most practical treatment, because when the lettering is to be outlined it is not necessary to be as careful when sizing the letters. Often the edges of some of the letters will be a little ragged where the leaf has not adhered completely, particularly when the truck surface has been powdered. An outline will clean up these places.

Keep outlines narrow on truck lettering. When outlines are heavy, they steal the show away from the gold, which should be the dominant material. Narrow outlines not only look smarter, they are easier to execute than heavy lines. A three-inch letter should not have an outline wider than one-sixteenth of an inch; smaller letters, proportionately narrower.

The use of gold leaf as an outline around a colored center makes some striking effects on trucks (Figures 118, 119 and 120). On a red truck, for example, a white center with gold outline is smart and attractive. On a dark blue truck, a gold outline around vermilion centers is a possibility. Similar combinations often look good on some of the pastel colors and white, against which gold alone does not show well. When outlining colored centers

**Figure 119.** "Kyanize Paints" was done with gold outlines and vermilion centers. Lettering on the door is plain gold with a narrow vermilion outline. "Glendora" is plain gold with no ornamentation. The truck is medium dark blue.

**Figure 120.** Using a solid paint color and replacing a logo color. The balance of the lettering is in spun gold. The entire door and panel were sprayed with two-component urethane to protect the gold.

in gold, it is best to use bold letter styles and to make the outline quite heavy so that it shows well. Spinning the gold enhances the effectiveness of the outline.

On logos and insignias that are done in colors, the use of a narrow gold outline to separate the areas of color adds richness. (This can also be used on signboards.)

Highlights are often used in combination with shading. A highlight is a fine outline of white, ivory, cream or lemon yellow made on the two sides of the letter strokes opposite the shade. A highlight is very effective in "picking up" the lettering when it is seen from angles from which the leaf itself shows dark.

Shading can range from the simple and quick off-shade separated only slightly from the letter to elaborate split shades, surface toning for three dimensional effects and two-tone underblending (i.e., with asphaltum) that can take a lot of time. In many cases a short feature line can be dressed up with these more elaborate effects, and the extra time spent doing this can be made up by cutting corners on the balance of the lettering. This is a good treatment for heavy copy or for a business style that warrants the extra ornamentation.

**Varnish**    In finishing a truck job, a question arises concerning the use of varnish. Many feel that gold leaf loses much of its natural, rich luster when given a

122          Gold Leaf Techniques/*Truck Gilding*

final coat of varnish, particularly when used for outdoor signs. The effect on the brilliance of the gold is much the same as that produced by rubbing. Varnish diffuses the reflected light and dulls the gild somewhat. However, highly burnished, unvarnished gold can appear almost black when seen from certain angles. This is especially true on truck doors, where lettering is low and on a receding surface.

Although varnishing induces cracking and peeling, particularly in areas of the country with high temperatures, these disadvantages are outweighed by the protection varnish gives the gilded surface. Trucks are subjected to a lot of friction from scraping through tree branches and shrubbery, from road splashes, fuel spills, and from washing with strong solutions and high-pressure washes. If the lettering is not varnished, it loses its luster and turns dark after a few months on an average truck. Often only the bare size remains after a year's service. Such an experience may cause a customer to decide to forgo gold in favor of paint on his next truck.

The best material to use is Chromatic Clear Overcoat Varnish, which is an alkyd resin and kin to the automotive clears we are all familiar with. You can brush the varnish over the lettering or spray the entire area, whichever is most practical for the job. This is best done after the size is dry, at the earliest on the next day; better yet, wait two or three days if possible.

# Other Surface Gilding Applications

**Office Doors**  A sign painter called upon to execute gold lettering on office doors will find himself facing a variety of surfaces, from glass to wood—either painted or varnished—and even metal (Figure 121). Whatever the material, gold lettering on an office door is much richer and more dignified than lettering done in paint.

An office door fitted with clear glass is an invitation to the sign painter to sell a regular glass gilding job, of course, but surface gilding is often done on such doors. When the glass is frosted or prismatic, then any gold lettering must be done by surface-gilding methods. The procedure is much the same as gilding done on a truck or signboard with quick sizes. If the job is small, rubbing varnish can be used for size and will be ready to gild in ten to fifteen minutes, but longer jobs will require a slower size, such as synthetic quick size, Venice size, or lettering enamel size.

When surface gilding is done on a glass door, the size should be colored with black, so that the lettering will be opaque when completed. Only a small amount of black need be used. It is not necessary that the size be opaque itself, as the combination of the dark-colored size with the leaf will render the lettering solid enough. Use either oil or bulletin color; do not use japan color.

When gilding on rapid-drying size such as rubbing varnish, it is advisable to press the leaf well into the size before wiping off the loose gold. This is especially important in the case of lettering on glass, where every crack will show. This can be done with a hard ball of cotton, or better yet, with the ball of a finger or the heel of your palm.

Gold lettering on glass doors is generally finished with a black outline. Such outlining should be kept narrow. Terminals of the outline strokes can be trimmed with a razor blade, if desired, for neat corners. It is unusual to varnish over door lettering, as the glass in most office buildings is infrequently washed, but if the lettering is varnished it will be a longer-lasting job.

When gilding is done on varnished or painted doors, the usual precautions should be observed to make sure that leaf will not stick to the background. If the surface is tacky, dust it with talcum or rub it with a raw potato. The lettering can be outlined with black or any dark color, if the location seems to warrant it. For dark-colored doors a better choice might be white or yellow, or even to omit an outline altogether. Red outlines,

**Figure 121.** This office door lettering is gold with black outlines on natural wood.

which are popular on truck lettering, have no place on an office door. They are too flashy, as are other bright colors.

**Stone**
According to most literature, stone requires a priming coat before applying size in order to prevent suction, but many a sign painter unaware of this information blithely gilded on stone without any kind of surface preparation, using both slow and quick sizes, indoors and outdoors, and never had any trouble on marble or granite. It is possible that with other kinds of stone a priming coat might be necessary. In this case, burnishing sealer or undercoat primer should be used.

Surface gilding on polished stone is often found on directories and directional signs for hallways of public buildings, memorial tablets, etc. (Figure 122). It is easy to do and looks smart. Either slow size or quick size can be used and the procedure is the same as for any ordinary type of surface gilding. Lettering can be trimmed with a razor blade, as on glass, if the blade is used at a rather flat angle and renewed often. Old lettering can be removed with the razor blade or by using solvents such as lacquer thinner or paste paint remover.

Gold lettering on light-colored stone can be outlined in black. On darker stones it is better to leave the lettering plain.

The sign painter is also called at times to gild letters incised in stone. This presents some special difficulties, not the least of which is pushing the leaf into the narrow crevices. For this work a slow size is best. It should be gilded before it is too dry for good retention of leaf. Before applying size, be sure to clean out the bottoms of the cuts in the stone, as they usually have a certain amount of sand or powdered stone in them. Apply the size as

125

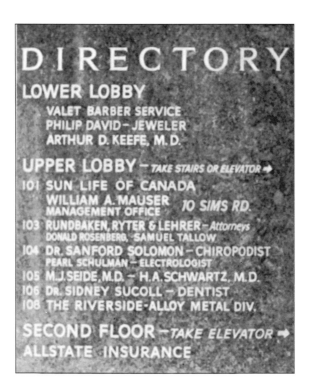

**Figure 122.** Surface gold lettering on polished granite. Small lettering (tenants' names) is ⅝ in. high. Terminals were trimmed with razor blade.

thinly as possible; otherwise it will run and form puddles that will cause trouble during gilding.

Gilding incised letters is a matter of laying pieces of leaf repeatedly on the surface and pushing them into the depressions until the letters are completely covered. This is best done with a badger shaving brush or soft fitch, as described in Chapter 5. The same brush is used to clean out the loose gold and to smooth the gild, since rubbing with cotton or velvet is obviously out of the question. (This same procedure can be used to gild letters incised in wood, described in Chapter 6.)

It is difficult to apply size neatly in incised lettering without getting a certain amount on the surface. On stone with a rough surface, that cannot be easily cleaned later, all you can do is size as neatly as possible. But when sizing letters incised in polished stone, it isn't necessary to be careful. Slop the size on the surface as much as you like, and when the gilding is complete, clean off the excess by rubbing the surface with a cuttle bone (Figure 123). Cuttle bone, used by caged birds to sharpen their beaks, can be obtained at any pet supply store. It is abrasive enough so that it removes the excess gild like magic, yet is soft enough that it does not scratch the stone. It is so soft that it wears rapidly and thus constantly presents a clean surface to the work. Incidentally, a razor blade is no good for this work, since it will catch on the rough edges and become useless in seconds.

## Porous Surfaces

Any surface that absorbs gold size to any extent has to be sealed before successful gilding can be done. This includes paper and cardboard, new plaster, wallboard (drywall), surfaces painted with some water-based paints, and others. The sealing doesn't need to be done over the entire surface. It is only necessary to seal the letter form and follow with size.

Gold Leaf Techniques/*Other Surface Gilding Applications*

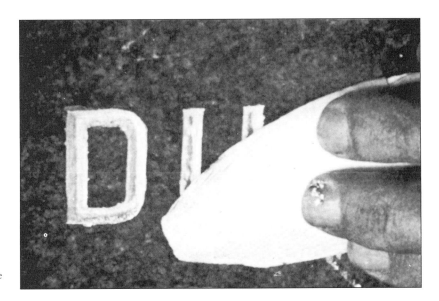

**Figure 123.** Excess size is cleaned from the surface of stone by rubbing with a cuttle bone.

Your favorite gold size makes a satisfactory sealer by itself on most porous surfaces, so the job is simply a matter of applying two coats of size. Allow the first coat to dry thoroughly before going over it with the second coat. In extreme cases, a third coat may be necessary. You can tell by the appearance of the second coat. It is ready to gild when the size sets up with a uniform, glossy finish. However, since drying time can be critical, sealing might be better done with a faster-drying finish than the size, so that you will be able to size sooner. Use fast-drying block-out white, primer mixtures, or burnishing sealer.

## Burnished Gilding on Smooth Surfaces

Occasionally it is necessary to execute a gold-leaf design on glass that will appear burnished from both sides or to produce burnished gilding on china and similar articles. There are various methods for doing this. One old-time stunt that has been told around sign shops (and that works, too) is the following: Gild on the front surface with water size, just as in ordinary glass gilding. Paint the design on top of the leaf with asphaltum. When the asphaltum is dry, clean off the excess leaf with water and Bon Ami, as in regular glass gilding, then wash off the asphaltum with turpentine. This will leave the design in burnished gold on the surface. A coat of varnish can be applied if desired, but this will dull the luster of the gold to some extent. Ordinary back-up paint can be used instead of using asphaltum, but it must be cleaned off before the paint is too dry. You may need to use lacquer thinner to clean off the paint.

When the job is not a rush order, a much simpler method for use on china or opaque objects (where it isn't necessary for the burnished leaf to be seen from both sides) is simply to do the inscription with slow size applied very thin and let it become practically dry before applying the leaf. This will produce a high luster almost the equal of that obtained with water-size gilding.

You can also gild with water size, then paint the design on top of the gold with clear rubbing varnish. The job is complete and already varnished as soon as the leaf is cleaned off. This method can be used for window pictorials that are designed to be seen from both inside and outside.

**Figure 124.** Gold lettering on drum head. The gold has a spun effect. Top line has black outline and shade, plus an additional split shade of light blue. Bottom line has black outline only.

These methods are not to be compared with the process of firing the gild into the surface of glass or ceramic materials, which produces gilded designs that are infinitely more durable. The methods given here will not withstand being immersed in water for any length of time. However, they may be useful for gilding on glass or china articles intended for purely decorative use.

**Aluminum and Other Metals**

Gilded metal objects, such as weather vanes and caducei for outdoor service, need a finish to protect them from corrosion before they are sized. A gold size by itself will not be sufficient. Aluminum presents a special problem in that primers satisfactory for other metals will not always adhere well to aluminum. DuPont's aluminum automotive preparation, which has its own specific pre-treatment and primer, is the best to use. Zinc chromate is usually used as a primer on aluminum after pre-treatment and can also be used on copper, bronze, prepared steel and sheet metal. Iron or cold rolled steel needs to be primed with a rust-preventive metal primer.

Lead is a metal that does not corrode or oxidize to any extent and therefore needs little surface preparation other than a good cleaning before being sized and gilded. Scrubbing with steel wool will clean the surface of lead adequately and at the same time provide a tooth for the retention of the size.

**Drumheads**

The use of gold leaf for the lettering or insignia on a drum will give it that extra something that will make it catch the eye in a parade or on the field (Figure 124). It is also quite an uncomplicated process.

When a drumhead is made of real leather, it is an ideal surface to letter with paint of any kind. Gilding ordinarily requires no surface preparation. Just size with your favorite quick size and gild. Spinning the gold is very effective. Outlining or shading can be done with oil, japan or bulletin colors. Whatever kind of paint is used, it will never peel. Lettering can be varnished if desired, but usually this isn't considered necessary. The only precaution that need be taken is to apply paint very thinly over large areas, or it can make the drum useless by dulling the resonance almost completely.

Occasionally one comes across a troublesome skin. Some of the cheaper drumheads may have rough spots that are porous and will need two coats of size. This condition can be detected easily enough by the fact that the size will dry dull in those areas.

Should you be required to remove old lettering from a drumhead, you will be in for quite a session, because paint adheres so firmly. Don't try to use solvent of any kind, as you will only succeed in driving the color deeper into the skin. The only practical method is to scrape the lettering off with a razor blade held at right angles to the skin. Follow by sanding with fine sandpaper. Finally, apply a thin coat of sealer, such as X-I-M Flash Bond or Chromatic Primer Sealer, and sand again lightly. This can usually be done without any serious damage to the drumhead, but it is wise to make a disclaimer beforehand for any possible damage. The scraping and sanding will leave the skin rough, so that lettering won't be as easy as on a new head. Don't quote too low on these jobs.

When a drumhead is made of a synthetic material such as vinyl or polymerized plastic, use the directions for vinyl in the next section.

## Vinyl and Imitation Leather

Most imitation leathers are vinyl, and adhesion is a difficulty easily overcome with *Enam-L-Koat*, made by Best Buy Banner Co. A thin coat applied with a rag and allowed to dry will permit adhesion of any paint or gold size to the vinyl material. It can be used on any color, as it dries clear.

Imitation leathers with an embossed pattern require thick gold size that will not puddle in the embossing. A mixture that will remain flexible is the best choice. (See "Sizes" Chapter 5.)

Gilding on vinyls opens up possibilities for work on tire covers, golf bags, instrument cases, drumheads, vinyl banners, awnings, and the like.

## Etched and Glue-Chipped Glass

The easiest process for gilding glue-chipped glass is to first gild with water size. This size should be slightly stronger than usual, by perhaps one-half capsule, in order to flow onto the ridges of the chip. Care must be taken to allow all of the size to flow out of the chip to avoid puddles. When the size is dry, a light rub-down is necessary to keep the chip from cutting much of the gild. There will inevitably be holidays—go over these with clear varnish or oil size, which will stick better to the ridges than water size. This will not detract from the appearance, since large portions of the lettering will always show as a matte gild anyway (Figure 125).

Figures 126 and 127 show sandblasted glass gilded with oil size. While it is possible to gild with water, the pebble finish of the etched glass will result in a matte finish to the gild. Therefore, gild with clear oil size, waiting as long as possible in order to achieve a more complete gild and a good burnish when viewed from the other side.

## Carrara Glass Tablets

Black or dark-colored Carrara glass, frequently used in store front installations, makes beautiful and practical directory tablets for office buildings and many

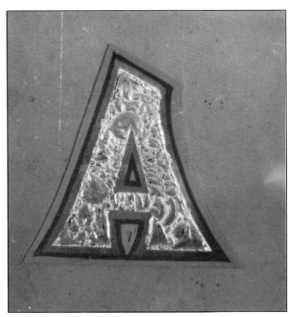

**Figure 125.** Glue-chipped glass letter, gilded with double outlines. Note that portions of the letter appear matte.

**Figure 126.** The Masonic emblems in this door were sandblasted into the glass and gilded in two tones of gold leaf. Sandblasting was done from the inside.

other applications when surface-gilded. This material is more substantial than ordinary plate glass, being $^{11}/_{32}$ of an inch thick. It is made with a highly polished and very flat surface.

Lettering is done by ordinary surface-gilding methods and can be

**Figure 127.** Detail of individual square from door pictured in Figure 126. Compass and letter G are gilded with XX gold; square is gilded with lemon gold. Clear oil size was used so that the design appears normal from either side.

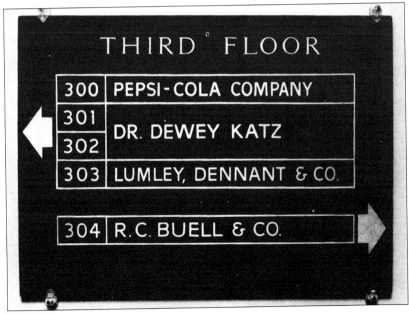

**Figure 128.** A black carrara glass directory tablet with surface gold lettering. Installation is with plastic clips built up to thickness of the glass with cork.

trimmed with a razor blade after gilding. Ordinarily, the lettering isn't outlined on signs of this type. In fact, outlining would destroy their rich simplicity. The lettering should be varnished, however, as protection against scratching.

Building owners and superintendents like these directories because of the ease with which changes are made (Figure 128). It is only necessary to scrape off a name with a razor blade and proceed immediately with the new lettering. The whole process can be a one-trip job if not done in the shop.

Erection is simple if you use the plastic clips that are commonly used for mirror installations. Since these clips are made for the standard quarter-inch thickness, you will have to use a washer or similar device to accommodate the thicker Carrara glass.

A good glass shop can cut this glass into most any shape for use as awards, logo plates, or the like. Find a supplier who has some used Carrara, and you may have a source for some unusual tablets.

A more permanent type of sign can be made with Carrara glass by having the inscription sandblasted into the glass and then filling the lettering with gold leaf. The sandblasting needn't be too deep, only about a sixteenth of an inch or so. If you are not set up to do your own sandblasting, this work can be done by most monument concerns. You will want to do the masking yourself in order to have some control over the quality of the design. Gild sandblasted glass as you would lettering incised in stone, using slow oil size.

## Gold Leaf Lettering on Boats

Most boats today are made of fiberglass, and some surface preparation should be made. When the fiberglass is molded, a release agent is used in order to remove it from the mold. This agent must be removed before sizing. The best solution to use is DuPont 3812S Reducer, wiped over the area with a soaked rag and dried with clean cloths. It has been my experience that two or three cleanings are necessary to prepare the surface completely. If the surface appears to be particularly slick or has any indications of an oily substance, pre-wash the area with DuPont Prep-Sol, then 3812S. Trichoroethane can be used instead of 3812S, but it doesn't seem to provide as much tooth in the surface. Gilding is done the same as for trucks, taking into account the variables of the area and weather conditions.

If you are called to do a wooden boat, beware of the finish. Often the boats are re-varnished with marine spars, which are slow driers, and consequently sticking may be a problem. Use the methods mentioned for this problem in Chapter 6. Egg size is the best solution, since boats tend to have heavier coats of uncured varnish, making for the worst sticking problem ever.

Needless to say, gilding boats can be done better on dry land, away from any possible contamination from water spray or heavy condensation.

Be aware of state and federal regulations regarding sizes and styles for lettering on boats.

 # Miscellaneous and Tricks of the Trade

**Planning Sizes of Gold Lettering**

When laying out jobs to be done in gold leaf, whether on windows, trucks, or any other surface, keep in mind that the leaf measures just a little over three inches and, wherever possible, make the height of the letters close to multiples of this measurement. It is barely possible to gild letters that are a full three inches high with one leaf. Cutting the size down just an eighth of an inch allows you a much greater margin of safety. If the letter is made a quarter of an inch over three inches, you won't be able to place the leaf exactly enough to gild the line with the width of the leaf, and you will use much more gold. A letter one and one-quarter inch high is about the limit that can be gilded practically with half leaves.

The same principles apply in planning the width of strokes on large letters.

**More About Pounce Patterns**

In glass gilding nothing makes the job go as smoothly as having a good, accurate pattern to work from, and any additional time spent in refining the pattern is sure to be made up during the operations on the glass. The time saved on the job can be as much as double the time required to make a pattern. This is especially true when lettering is to be backed up in outline only. Many sign painters have bragged in the past about the fact that they don't need a good pattern to work from. This is empty talk, particularly if you desire to produce the good quality of craftsmanship that gold leaf deserves. Anyone can do glass work without a pattern, but they will do a superior job, in less time, when they have a good pattern to work from.

The illustrations in this book show patterns being made with a pounce wheel. However, a gilder who wishes to do accurate work should seriously consider the purchase of an electric perforator, which will consistently prepare a good line and a clean hole through which an even amount of powder can be deposited. An electric perforator is only one of the many tools we can use to simplify the work involved in good gold leaf. Don't hesitate to use such mechanical aids as straightedges, triangles, compasses, ellipsographs, dividers and the like, especially during the perforating operation. The lettering can be drawn freehand and perforated accurately with such aids.

Figures 129 and 130 show a good procedure for perforating a line of lettering using a four-foot straightedge and a draftsman's adjustable triangle to produce strokes of script and italic lettering with exactly the same slant.

133

**Figure 129.** Use of draftsman's triangle to perforate vertical strokes. Triangle rests against a 4 foot straightedge, which is moved for each line of lettering.

The diagonal strokes of letters such as A, M, W, and Y, can be made equal on both sides merely by flipping this tool over after the correct angle has been set. A pounce wheel or perforating wand fitted into a beam compass (wood variety for the electric perforator, of course) makes the perforating of larger circles easy and exact. These are difficult to perforate accurately if done freehand, yet if large circles are not done accurately on the pattern, they are a true hazard when the brush work is done. Not being able to rely on the pattern, the brush work is tedious and uncertain.

When the pattern is pounced on the gild to back it up, hills and valleys of powder will produce a ragged edge in the backing paint. Art Sarti, in the second edition of this book, suggested squeegeeing over the inscription to smooth out the powder. Place a sheet of paper or cardstock over the inscription, being careful not to mar the gild, and squeegee over the back. This will smooth out the pounce powder and pick up some of the excess (Figure 131).

Described below are only a few of the many shortcuts to making patterns.

Even though the job requires that several lines of lettering be centered on the pattern, do not try to center them when you draw them, but let the ends come where they will. Mark the center point of each line. When perforating, lay a new piece of paper under the pattern you have drawn and, as each line is perforated, shift the top pattern one way or the other to center the line on the bottom paper. The bottom pattern then is used as the working pattern.

Gold Leaf Techniques/*Miscellaneous and Tricks of the Trade*

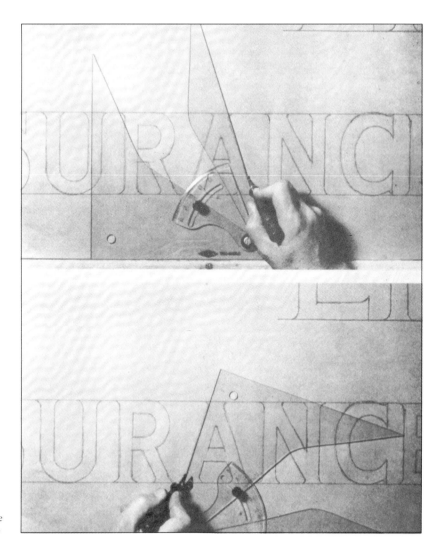

**Figure 130.** Use of the adjustable triangle. Both sides of the letter A are perforated at exactly the same angle by flipping the triangle.

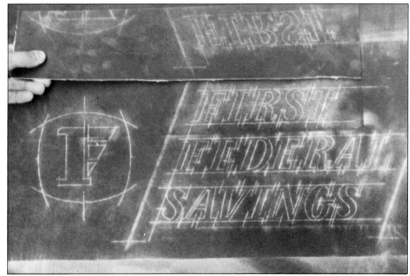

**Figure 131.** Squeegee over the pounced area to flatten out any hills that might interfere with backing. In this photograph only the word "First" has been squeegeed. Note that it is just as legible as the unsqueegeed copy below it.

Figure 132. Duplicating letters by tracing. The letter C at left was first traced on tracing paper, which was then placed in position and held in place while a carbon sheet was slipped under it.

Tracing can be used to advantage in pattern making. It is foolish to draw intricate letters such as G, O, and S more than once, particularly if you want all of them to match. After drawing the first one, trace this and transfer it with carbon paper to those places where the same letter occurs again (Figure 132). Another way of transferring the letter is to perforate through the tracing for the second impression. Very few can draw a perfectly symmetrical letter O.

When you want a particularly nice O draw the letter on a piece of tracing paper. Mark horizontal and vertical dividing lines through the center. Select that quarter of the letter which seems to be the most perfect and transfer it four times onto the pattern for a perfect letter. Other complicated symmetrical shapes can be done in the same manner. When these are large, they can be transferred from one half of the pattern to the other simply by folding the pattern through the center of the design and perforating through the two halves.

When making a pattern for a glass job that is to be backed up in outline only, as for the usual sort of matte center work, any variation in the widths of individual letter strokes become very noticeable in the widths of the centers. Don't guess at the widths of the strokes, but use dividers or a rule to make the strokes of uniform width throughout (Figure 133). (Note: the horizontal strokes in plain letters are supposed to be a trifle narrower than the vertical strokes.)

Some jobs require detail that is too small to be perforated accurately with a pounce wheel. The point of the electric perforator can be sharpened on a grinding wheel for this type of pattern. In the absence of an electric perforator, you may even resort to perforating these details with a common pin held in a pin vise. This is not as time-consuming as it might sound if all the straight lines are perforated against a straightedge. Circles can be perforated with dividers, if a hard support is provided for the center leg to prevent the point from digging in and making such a large hole that accuracy is destroyed. A small piece of plastic sheet under the center point will help.

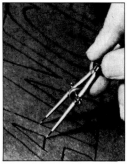

Figure 133. Use dividers to make letter strokes uniform. This is being done just prior to perforating.

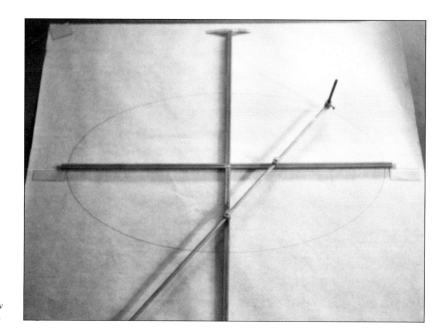

**Figure 134.** The Brunskill Ellipsograph, set up to draw an ellipse on pattern paper.

Drafting supply houses carry a tool called a horn center for this purpose.

Carbon paper can be used to transfer fine detail to light-colored surfaces. Plain paper smeared with chalk or whiting on the back can be used on dark-colored surfaces. The pattern in these cases is not perforated. It is placed in position on the working surface, the carbon paper is slipped underneath, and the design is traced. A very clean impression will result if the tracing is done with a fine-point pen. This method is very useful for transferring monograms or other small designs onto cars and trucks. It can also be employed for transferring a design to the back of gold leaf on glass. Dressmakers' carbon paper, found in yard goods stores, comes in larger sheets and different colors for use on different surfaces.

An excellent material for making patterns is 30- or 40-pound wrapping paper. White paper can also be used as a sun shade, as mentioned in Chapter 2. Kraft paper (brown) is cheaper and makes good patterns as well. Both have a good surface to draw upon, perforate well, and are strong, which is an advantage when making patterns that will have continued and frequent use. Patterns made with lighter-weight papers often sold for this purpose are a waste of effort, since a good pattern is so important to the quality of the job.

## Drawing Ellipses

There are two methods for drawing accurate ellipses, and both are worthy of mention. First and simplest is to purchase an ellipsograph. Many are marketed, the best known being the *OvalCompass* and *The Brunskill Elipsograph* (Figure 134). They are basically a mechanical axis with accompanying apparatus to draw an ellipse of any dimension. They are far and away the best and most accurate method of drawing ellipses and elliptical shapes.

Until your operation can justify the purchase of such a tool, ellipses can be constructed with a loop of string. Most pattern makers are familiar with the method of drawing ellipses with a loop of string tied around two pins, but the method for locating these two focuses for a given length and

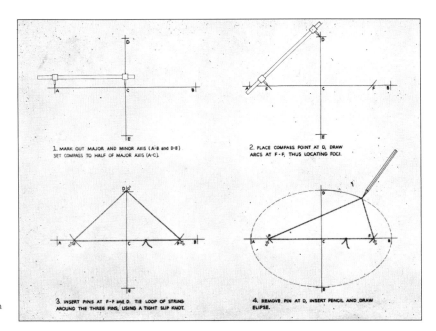

1. MARK OUT MAJOR AND MINOR AXIS (A-B and D-E) SET COMPASS TO HALF OF MAJOR AXIS (A-C).

2. PLACE COMPASS POINT AT D, DRAW ARCS AT F-F, THUS LOCATING FOCI.

3. INSERT PINS AT F-F and D. TIE LOOP OF STRING AROUND THE THREE PINS, USING A TIGHT SLIP KNOT.

4. REMOVE PIN AT D, INSERT PENCIL AND DRAW ELLIPSE.

**Figure 135.** Constructing an ellipse with a loop of string.

width of ellipse is not as commonly known. Figure 135 illustrates the entire procedure. It is based upon the geometrical principle that the sum of the distances from any point on the ellipse to the two focuses is constant and equal to the major axis. The loop of string provides a mechanical means of maintaining this condition, as can be seen from a little study of the drawing.

The work will be more accurate if some type of string having very little stretch is chosen for this operation. Heavy shoemaker's thread is an excellent choice.

It is possible to use this method to construct two or more concentric ellipses. The same two pin locations, however, cannot be used. It is necessary to relocate the focuses for each ellipse. (The term "concentric" used is not mathematically exact; in this connection we mean drawing two ellipses, one within the other, so that the distance between the two curves appears equal all around.) Using an ellipsograph is a much better way to get multiple concentric ellipses.

## Scoring Circles for Glass Gilding

A simple tool similar to the one pictured in Figures 136 and 137 can be used to easily produce perfect circles in gold leaf on glass. A similar tool can be fabricated from a yard stick and produces a suitable radius. This is an enhancement of the line scoring technique discussed earlier but applied to circles. Begin by gilding the area for the circle or concentric circles in the usual manner. In the center, fasten a suction cup that has an attached bolt. The scoring tool can now be attached to the bolt and the circles scored with the pointed, wet wood dowel as pictured. Any number of circles can be scored in this manner, and they will be made much more accurately than with a bow compass. Make sure that the score line is clean and wide enough so that clear rubbing varnish used for backing-up can cover the score line and not be seen. This technique was followed by Art Sarti for the seals shown in Figure 138.

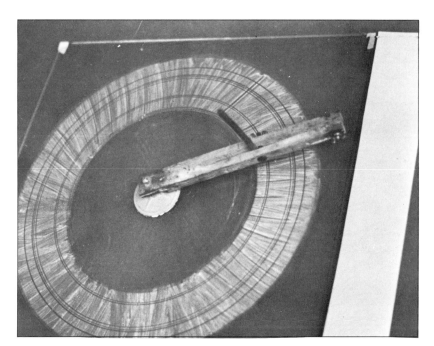

Figure 136. A custom-made compass for scoring circles.

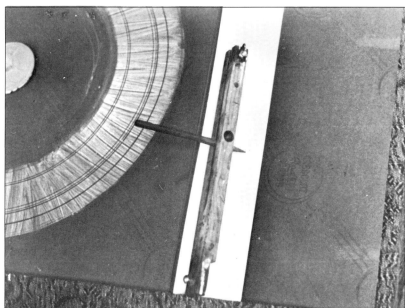

Figure 137. The hardwood scoring tool is held in place with a bolt and wing nut.

## Oil Color Pigments

The section on glass gilding refers to the use of high-grade pictorial oil colors, particularly Prussian blue. Following is a list of other useful oil colors (not necessarily the only colors available in oil).

**Cadmium Colors**

Light and medium yellow, orange, and deep red. All have exceptional hiding ability and are fade-resistant. Cadmium colors are slow to dry, so mix with vehicles accordingly.

**Phthalo Blue and Green**

(Phthalocyanine, "phthalo" for short) Very transparent and somewhat stiff-working, but make brilliant tints for white and are absolutely permanent. A

139

**Figure 138.** The seals of the United States, the state of Arizona, and the President of the United States.

virtue of the phthalo colors is that they can be mixed freely with all other pigments without danger of chemical reaction. To make a brilliant and solid-covering, permanent emerald green, mix phthalo green with cadmium yellow light and white.

**Ivory Black**  A member of the lampblack family and more solid-covering than other blacks, useful in mixing with japan black for lettering office doors and any other application requiring an extremely solid black. Also used for tinting smalt paint.

**Earth Colors**  Yellow ochre, raw sienna, burnt sienna, raw umber and burnt umber. All are absolutely permanent and very useful in combination with gold, with which they blend harmoniously. Burnt sienna and burnt umber mixed with generous portions of varnish make good glazing colors for surface shading on gold leaf when asphaltum is not available or practical. Yellow ochre, raw sienna, and burnt sienna are useful for tinting white to make pleasing and non-darkening creams and buffs.

**Alizarin Crimson**  A very transparent, cool, dark red, useful in combination with phthalo blue and white for making reasonably permanent purples and lavenders or with white alone to yield delicate shades of pink.

**Quinacridone Red**  A deep scarlet red with good color retention, the reddest of the reds. It can be used by itself and mixes with other colors in clean combinations. This is a good base for carmine and maroons when mixed with phthalo or Prussian blue. Can be mixed to fire red with yellow or orange.

**Cobalt Violet**  Brilliant and absolutely permanent, but transparent. It should be undercoated with a more solid-covering color of approximately the same shade. Good glazing color on aluminum leaf.

If you have difficulty in obtaining pictorial oil colors, the better grades of artists' oil colors such as Winsor & Newton can be used, although they fade faster. Do not use synthetic colors. An analysis on the label will help you determine if the pigments are pure and not extended. Some colors contain a small percentage of aluminum stearate as an anti-separation agent, which does no harm. The purer the pigment, the better durability it will have. If your supplier does not carry pictorial oil colors, contact the manufacturer direct. Chromatic and Dana Classic brands are both recommended.

**Varnishes**

Throughout the book I have referred to various varnishes that are to be used in gilding. Use the following list as an easy reference and explanation of various types of varnish.

**Spar**

(Sometimes called bulletin spar) Originally available in pure form and used for general mixing with pigment and for clear-coating. Most spar varnishes now are based in urethane and are referred to as plastic varnishes. They are not as brushable when mixed with pigment, but are generally good for clear-coating. Most are slightly yellow in color, though they do not turn much darker. Durability of these finishes varies by brand and should be tested individually.

**Water-White Window Spar**

Similar in characteristic to spar varnishes, but formulated to remain absolutely clear (white). Some of the newer urethane bases will not stick well to glass and are easily removed with window-cleaning compounds. For varnishing gold on glass, overcoat clear has superior durability.

**Quick Rubbing**

Originally formulated to be used on wood to give a hand-rubbed appearance with the protective qualities of a varnish resin. When single-coated on wood, the finish is usually alcohol-proof, which makes it ideal for furniture. For sign work, quick rubbing varnish is used as a binder for pigments, usually japan colors. It is the main ingredient in back-up color for glass gilding and can be used by itself for this purpose. Drying time for clean-up is about fifteen to twenty minutes, with a cure time of twenty-four hours. It is reduced only with turpentine and often remains self-solvent after curing.

**Fibroseal (Also "Liqui-Seal")**

A synthetic, quick-drying, mixing varnish. Very thin in body, it is added as additional binder to paints and varnish mixes and can be used as a thinner for backing color made with rubbing varnish and japan color. It also makes an excellent bronzing fluid. Black Fibroseal is the same varnish, pre-mixed with black pigment for lettering purposes usually popular for office doors and shades or outlines on gold leaf.

**Quick Gold Size**

A relative of the japan varnishes, sometimes used as a binder for pigments, it is more frequently used as a gold size and will gild in one to three hours.

**Venice Japan (Gold Size)**

Good-quality gold size that is ready to gild in about one hour. It reaches a tack and burnish similar to that of slow size that has set for a few days; however, it should only be used for small inscriptions, since there is very little time to gild once proper tack is reached. Use only for inscriptions that can be gilded in ten to fifteen minutes.

**Florence Japan**

Highest-grade japan varnish in purity, mixability and durability. The fastest gold size, ready to gild in one hour with the same properties of quick size. Used as a binder with pigments and as a thinner in back-up color. When mixed with japan colors, thinned with turpentine, can be used for paper signs and will dry flat in fifteen minutes.

| | |
|---|---|
| **Damar** | Clear, natural resin-based, turpentine-solvent varnish used primarily for matte effects and embossed effects in glass gilding and as an adhesive for trick centers. It is a very thick-bodied varnish, and a small amount will cover a large area after proper mixing. Quick rubbing varnish should be added as a hardener, frequently with an additional dryer. It can be added to other varnishes, such as japans, to enhance gloss. |
| **Overcoat Clear** | Synthetic, alkyd resin varnish formulated as a top-coat sealer and modified to adhere to truck finishes and glass. Excellent as a final varnish for glass gilding. Its mild solvent base reduces "lifting." It is thinned with a good grade of mineral spirits (not oleum) or flow extenders and can be used as a binder for pigments, preferably oil colors. |
| **Saving Scrap Gold Leaf** | Skewings may amount to quite a lot of gold in a year's time and may be saved in the old-fashioned skewing box most readers may have seen at one time or another. This is simply a wooden box that has in its lid a large opening covered with wide-mesh (one-quarter-inch), wire screen material. This is handy for scraping gold skewings off the cotton that is used for wiping gilded work in the shop. Gold skewings from truck lettering jobs done away from the shop can be collected in an envelope and brought back to the shop. If the loose gold can be wiped off without first being pressed into the size, practically all the loose gold can be recovered. If the gold needs to be pushed into the size before wiping, a lot of it will land on the floor. |
| | It is hardly worth bothering to pick up and save the loose gold that is wiped from water-size gilding on glass, but the cotton that is used to clean off excess leaf after backing-up can be saved for the gold that it contains. This will amount to one-half to nine-tenths of all the gold laid on the glass. |
| | The reclaimable value of scrap gold has been about fifteen percent of the cost of an equivalent weight of leaf. You must decide whether your labor in saving and recycling the skewings is worth what you will get from reclaiming the gold. There is no point in saving silver or aluminum scrap unless these materials are used in really impressive quantities. |
| **Kit Containers** | It is obviously impossible for one to carry in one's kit the standard pint (or larger) cans for all the different materials that might be needed for different kinds of work. For carrying various thinners and varnishes for mixing, use half-pint kit cans, square or round, depending on where in the kit they will best fit. Liquid colors, varnishes, and gold sizes work well in two-ounce and four-ounce glass jars. Both of these sizes can be bought in case lots and are not expensive. They take up little room in the kit and keep the materials fresh, since they can be closed tightly. When a new can of varnish or color is opened, fill a few jars or kit cans and put them on the shelf for a convenient supply of fresh material when needed. It is likely that these containers pay for themselves by eliminating the waste of material that might form a skin in a larger can, in which case the convenience that they afford is free. When a jar or can is empty, don't bother to refill it, as it is better to throw it away and use a new one. The labeling detail is solved by painting a code letter or two on the cap or top. |
| | Sixteen-ounce, wide-mouthed jars are handy containers for rinsing brushes outside of the shop. When the contents get dirty, don't bother to clean them; throw them and the contaminants away, and use a new one. |

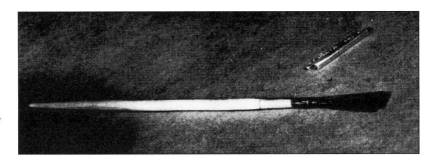

**Figure 139.** A quill properly fitted with a handle. Note how much of the quill has been cut off.

## Tape

Masking tape provides the most convenient way to hold patterns in place on windows, signboards and many other surfaces. (A tip from Bob Fitzgerald is to use magnets to hold patterns on steel truck bodies and signboards.) Use the better brands of tape that have good adhesive and are not crepe paper. The time saved by not having to reset tape that doesn't stick will more than compensate for the added expense.

For many years, sign painters have been using fine-line or low-tack tape to mark the top and bottom lines of copy to be lettered. This is a good way to get a clean line with regular lettering paints and can be used to get a good line on the bottom of a shade on glass work, but it will not work well with gold size. The tape leaves a ragged edge that will be repeated in the leaf. Of course you cannot tape across gold on glass, since it will pull the gold off in the most inconvenient places.

## Care of Brushes

The camel-hair quill brushes that are commonly used for lettering windows, trucks, and similar work usually come with attached handles. Occasionally you will find some French quills that are supplied without handles, which come separately. The common practice among sign painters has been to pick up whichever stick is handy, shove it into the quill and go to work. This provides about the poorest grip for a delicate tool that could possibly be devised, for it is exceedingly difficult to do fine work when the merest pressure makes the quill flop around in its handle. The following method for fitting quills to handles is also handy for adjusting ready-made quills to individual taste. This is best done before the quill is first oiled and applies to both real quills and those made of plastic. First soak the quill in boiling water, holding the brush by the hairs and being careful not to submerge any portion of the hair. The hot water will soften the quill and make it flexible. While it is soft, take a sharp knife and cut off the quill about three-quarters of an inch above the hair. Cut close enough so as to provide a section that is uniform in diameter, or nearly so, since the outer end of the natural quill will usually be smaller in diameter than the middle portion, making it difficult to fit a handle tightly. Plastic quills will need to be trimmed less, though they usually have a slight flare near the end that will need to be removed. Select a handle large enough to furnish a comfortable grip, yet proper for the size of the brush. Usually the handle should be larger in diameter than the quill of the brush. Whittle down the end of the stick so that it will fit snugly into the quill (Figure 139). Before inserting the handle again, dip the quill in the hot water so that it won't split. A drop of glue that will not be dissolved by paint solvents can be used to secure the handle. Either a hide glue or white glue works well if allowed to cure. Try fitting your next quill in this manner and see if it doesn't work more easily for you.

The hair of new quills should be oiled with a non-drying oil before being used in paint. This will fill the heel with oil so that paint will find it difficult to harden there. Lard oil is most commonly used for oiling brushes, though it presents some vermin problems in some areas and, by itself, does not combine with paint to prevent any residue from hardening in the brush. Castor oil is good in these two respects, but is heavy and difficult to work into the brush. Castor oil can be diluted with kerosene with excellent results, though the proper consistency is hard to maintain. A better mixture is made by adding one part lard oil to three parts castor oil that has been diluted with mineral oil. This mixture can be made in a large quantity and stored for use. Commercial brush treatment oils are also available which should be tested for suitability.

The following directions for cleaning and oiling brushes will help to prolong the longevity of a good brush. After use, wipe the paint out of the brush with a rag, then give the brush a good rinsing in solvent. In the shop, a gallon bucket allows for plenty of agitation, which helps to clean the brush. Rinse by submerging the brush in thinner and moving the handle up and down rapidly. This opens up the hair so that the rinsing action gets up into the heel and thoroughly cleans the brush. (Many sign painters advocate 100 strokes to ensure a thorough cleaning.) Wipe dry carefully, but do not apply enough pressure to actually pull the hairs from the quill or ferrule. Ultrasonic cleaners that will take solvents are available and will clean your brush very well, if not better than by hand. Be careful, though, to buy only a model made for flammable solvents, as they do generate heat and can burst into flames.

Keep brush oil in a container large enough to repeat this up-and-down action to force the oil well into the quill or ferrule. If you will try this method, you will be amazed how much paint comes out of the heel even after the brush has been thoroughly rinsed. To draw out more paint, you can clip the brush in position so that only the hairs float in the oil. Do not allow the hairs to rest on the bottom of the vessel, as this will bend them out of shape. On a new brush, press down on the hair in the bottom of the container and at the same time twirl the handle back and forth between the fingers. This gives an extra added measure of protection by spreading the hair into a fan on the bottom of the container and forcing additional oil into the heel (Figure 140). Do this several times, on both sides of the brush. Complete the treatment by pinching the hair against the edge of the container and squeezing out most of the oil, then straighten the hair and work the brush into proper shape before putting it away. How long does all this take? Less time than it takes to tell about it. It probably takes from 60 to 90 seconds per brush, a valuable investment for a valuable tool. You will find that you will need to change the oil as paint builds up in it.

The preceding may sound like pretty drastic treatment for a brush, and you won't be able to do this with an old brush. Any less effective method of cleaning and oiling will leave considerable paint in the heel, which will gradually harden and cause the brush to lose its spring. If the hair of a brush in this condition is spread out, the stiffened condition of the heel will prevent it from coming together again, and the brush immediately becomes useless.

**Figure 140.** Forcing oil into the heel of the brush.

If you begin this treatment on your new brushes, they will work beautifully for you until the tips of the hair are worn so badly that they will not make square corners any more.

Incidentally, the shedding of hair from a brush is something not generally understood. Many people erroneously believe that the hair is pulling out of the quill. Occasionally hair will come out of the quill of a badly-made brush, but when this is the case it usually comes out in bunches and not two or three at a time. When a brush sheds single hairs, you will usually find that they are either the same length as or shorter than the length of hair from tip to the quill. A new brush always contains quite a few short hairs that are not held by the binding, and these will come out one or two at a time for quite a while. Old brushes shed hair that break off at the heel. This is normal, and loss of a few hairs in this fashion is no cause for concern as there is always plenty of hair left. The process is accelerated and more detrimental if paint is allowed to dry in the heel. A stiffened heel is a more serious problem and will cause even more hair to break off.

Recommending brushes most suitable for glass work by brand name is not always helpful. In many cases, brand names of brushes are not names of makers, but rather of distributors, and their wares are likely to change as to origin many times in a short period. A safe guide as to quality is usually the price asked, for those who know good brushes are always willing to pay a premium price for quality.

In general, glass work requires quills a little longer and a little softer

145

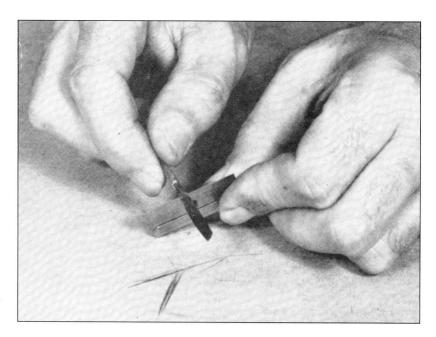

**Figure 141.** Cutting down a No. 3 quill to make a small outliner.

than for most other kinds of work, whereas lettering on rougher surfaces calls for shorter and springier brushes. Good brushes vary in length and in the spring of the hair. The requirements along these lines are an individual matter which all of us must decide for ourselves. Choosing a good brush is best accomplished in person since only a few in a bin of a particular size will suit each individual. A reputable mail order supplier will send a brush of good quality, but certain peculiarities that you may prefer will not necessarily be fulfilled.

Good outlining brushes are especially hard to come by. Longhair No. 2s and 3s (one and one-quarter to one and three-eighths inches long) often prove satisfactory for big work, but No. 0s and 1s rarely are suitable for small work. For fine outlining, cut down one-inch No. 2s to the required diameter. This is done by gently rotating the heel against a new razor blade (Figure 141). Do this very gently, as it is awfully easy to cut off all the hair this way. Cut down only new brushes, since old brushes somehow never seem to work properly when cut down. Almost any brush can be cut down in this manner to make a "half-size" when needed.

Sometimes a brush must be trimmed to length either to shorten it slightly or to even it up. Trimming more than one-sixty-fourth of an inch ruins the natural taper of the hairs and renders the brush useless. A slight trim, probably better measured in thousandths of an inch, will make a better brush out of a good brush. The best way to trim a brush is to fill it with oil and palette it out. Use a piece of glass with a straight, sharp edge. Allow the ends of the hairs to extend over the end of the glass just enough to trim, being careful not to allow the hairs to fan out of their normal shape. Run a piece of 200-grit sandpaper or an emery board vertically over the ends to cut the hairs off on the edge of the glass. Turn the brush over to do both sides. See Figure 142 for proper angle.

**Figure 142.** The proper method of trimming a brush on glass with sandpaper or an emery board. Note the angle at which the brush is held.

**Paper Cups**    Commercially produced paper bathroom cups are handy for mixing small quantities of fresh paint for each job and are easily discarded when done. They are wax-free and come in a three-ounce size with a handy dispenser for use in the shop. When used with a palette held underneath, they are lightweight and still allow you freedom to hold the mahl stick. Quite a quantity of these cups can easily be stacked in the corner of the kit.

**Making Paper Cups**    Figure 143 shows the steps involved in folding paint cups from envelopes or light cardstock. Since the lip is used for a palette while holding the mahl stick, many sign painters prefer them to three-ounce paper cups, and they are always handy when your stock of bathroom cups runs out. These cups are usually made from envelopes with 25-percent rag content so they won't leak paint or varnish. Cardstock will work as well. Keep some Number 10 envelopes or suitable cardstock in the glove compartment and elsewhere to have a good supply for emergencies.

**Hand-Held Size Pot**    Figure 144 shows Art Sarti's size pot, which allowed him to keep his size handy and all of his equipment in his left hand, close to the gilding area. Many don't like the added weight of the pot on the little finger, but some will find it saves a lot of reaching for the size brush from a table or ledge. The one pictured is a cheese spread jar that comes with a handle. Any pot with a bale handle will do; a wire handle can be attached to almost any pot.

**Making Palettes**    If you prefer to use a palette, Art Sarti suggested the following method using a card approximately 6″ x 10″; 14-ply show card material will do nicely (Figure 145). With a blade, cut out a hole for the thumb at the lower right side. In the center of the card, tape an empty gold leaf book to palette the brush on. Then, when one page loads with paint, merely turn another page. At the left of the palette, tape a paper cup with backing color. Next to the color you can clip a small cup with turpentine. While it is best to mix the backing

147

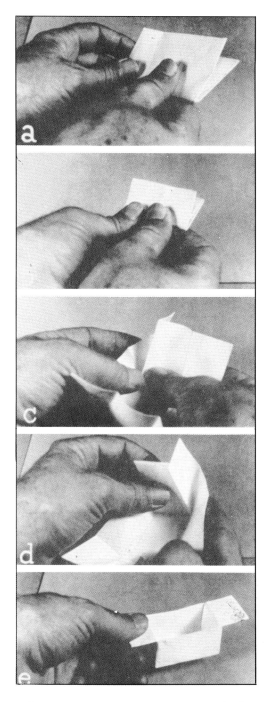

**Figure 143.** Making a paper cup from an envelope. (a) Fold in thirds crosswise, flap side out. (b) Without turning it over, again fold in thirds. (c) Open it up. Fit the corner creases one into the other as shown. Fold the diagonal ear around the end. (d) Repeat with all four corners. (e) The completed paint cup. It won't leak paint.

color to proper consistency, some prefer having turpentine handy to keep the palette wet. Mahl stick, palette, paint and thinner can all be held in one unit in the left hand while lettering with the free right hand. (Left-handers, please excuse the constant assumption that all sign painters are right-handed.)

**Figure 144.** The size pot is held with the small finger of the left hand.

**Figure 145.** A handmade palette ready for use.

**Figure 146.** The sign kit sitting on the end of the kit jacket. Note the opening for the sign kit handle.

## Sign Kit Jackets

Another practical gadget used for many years by Art Sarti is the sign kit jacket (Figure 146). Any sign painter with proper tools can make his own, or have a cabinetmaker make one. An important objective is to build the jacket so that it is sturdy enough to stand on or sit on, yet light enough so as to not add much weight to your kit.

Figure 147 clearly indicates the four shelf brackets and adjustable clips the sign kit sits on inside the jacket. The four sides are constructed of

149

**Figure 147.** The jacket, shown open, contains brackets and adjustable clips on which the sign kit rests.

one-half-inch overlaid plywood. The edges are dado-pinned and glued. The lid and bottom are five-eighths inch overlaid plywood with dado edges; the bottom is also pinned and glued. The lid rides on two hinges. The opening for the kit handle is about 1 ½″ x 6″. The latches on the opposite side from the lid hinges, lock the jacket securely. The latches on each side of the kit slide into channels on the inside of the jacket.

The inside measurements of this jacket are 16⅞″ x 9″. Stock kits may vary in size, so the cover should be constructed to fit the particular kit with which it is to be used. The height of the jacket illustrated is twelve inches, but this can vary depending on how much additional space you can make use of or desire between the bottom of the kit and the base of the jacket.

## Screen Printing Techniques for Gilding

In order to use screen printing to back up the gild, a knowledge of the techniques involved for making and using screens will be necessary. As with other phases of the sign business, screen printing can best be utilized when multiple copies of the same inscription are required. Letters smaller than one inch and complicated logos are also more accurately reproduced by screen printing using a stencil material that can be photographically produced.

For gilding on glass, proceed in the usual manner, using a pattern for the area to be backed up by the screen. The screen is held in place on the vertical window by using a horizontal or L-shaped support of wood at the bottom of the frame. This can be made to expand to wedge against the window frame on either side, or the vertical can be attached to the glass with double-stick foam tape. Once in proper registration, the frame itself can also be adhered to the glass in proper registration with foam tape. Obviously, it will be necessary to align the copy with the bottom edge of the frame during exposure to ensure proper registration on the glass.

For a backing paint, flat poster ink or Colonial Dekor gloss ink works most successfully. Chrome yellow is the toughest (as with japan colors), though black works quite well. The ink dries as fast as japan and cleans up well if done within twenty minutes. After clean-up, the screen can be reregistered in an off-set position for a shade. A sealer varnish of overcoat clear can be applied with a different screen or by hand.

Enamel size can be screened for surface applications and will be ready to gild in four to six hours. Use the same mixture as mentioned in Chapter 5, or extend enamel ink with mixing varnish to produce a size that will gild in about one hour.

Outlines for complicated work can be screened on the glass in black or other dark colors prior to gilding, as for upper-story window techniques. Dekor ink can be thinned to brushing consistency with turpentine and used for outlines or back-up in place of japan color though durability has not been proven.

**Imprints**  Do you wish to establish a reputation as a high-class signpainter? If the answer is "yes," execute every gold job in such a manner that you will be proud of it, and *sign* it...in gold, of course.

But—and it is a big but—it is easy to create the opposite impression if you are in the habit of making your imprint so large that it might be mistaken as the name of one of the partners in the firm that the sign is supposed to advertise. After all, it is an indication of superior ability to execute a small, neat imprint. Let's brag about our accomplishments without shouting. A small window inscription having letters up to two inches high ought to have an imprint no larger than one-sixteenth of an inch high. On larger spreads, an imprint can be a little bigger, but seldom more than three-sixteenths of an inch. On complicated inscriptions, the imprint can be worked in along a border or ornamentation. An imprint on an average truck should be about one-eighth of an inch high. That is large enough. Imprints on signboards should be large enough to be read from the sidewalk in front of the sign, but not from across the street!

# Appendix A
# Troubleshooting Guide

| Difficulty: | Cause: | Prevention: | Saving the job: |
|---|---|---|---|
| Size crawls on glass. | Glass insufficiently cleaned. Possibly wax or silicone on glass. | *Obvious. See page 12.* | *Re-clean the glass.* |
| | Size or size brush greasy. | *Obvious.* | *Clean pail and brush thoroughly and make fresh size.* |
| Leaf goes on wrinkled or cracked. | Not enough size on glass. | *Obvious.* | *No harm done except job will need more patching.* |
| | Too much air movement. | *Obvious.* | |
| | Leaf applied to glass too slowly. | *See page 22.* | |
| Leaf rubs off or develops numerous cracks when rubbed down with cotton after gilding. | Glass insufficiently cleaned. | *Obvious. See page 12.* | *No remedy except to start over again with clean glass.* |
| | Size too weak. | *See page 14.* | |
| | Rubbing too vigorously. | *Obvious.* | *No harm done.* |
| Leaf lifts with second application of size. | Glass insufficiently cleaned. | *Obvious.* | *No remedy.* |
| | Size too weak. | *Obvious.* | *Let job stand overnight.* |
| | Too much pressure with size brush or going over gild too many times. | *Obvious.* | *If washed-off spots not too large, patch and proceed.* |
| Can't see grease pencil lines through gold. | Dull day. Dark background. | *Pounce pattern.* | *Tack sheet of white paper over layout on outside of window.* |
| Can't see pounce lines against leaf on inside. | Lighting conditions not right. Wrong color pounce. | *Change pounce, install auxiliary side lighting.* | |
| Ragged or feather edges when backing up. | Paint too heavy or not enough varnish. | *Obvious.* | *Obvious.* |
| | Paint contains solid particles. | *Stir thoroughly or strain paint.* | |
| | Wrong brush. | *Use French soft camel hair quills.* | |

| Difficulty: | Cause: | Prevention: | Saving the job: |
|---|---|---|---|
| **Backing color runs into pounce lines causing ragged edge.** | Pounce lines too heavy. | *Small wheel, pounce lightly.* | *Blow off some of powder.* *Trim with razor blade.* |
| | Paint too thin. | *Obvious.* | |
| **Backing color chips when washing off surplus leaf.** | Color improperly mixed. | *See page 30, 31.* | |
| | Color not dry enough or too dry. | *See page 31.* | *Use gentle method of cleaning off leaf.* |
| | Too much water. | *See page 40.* | |
| | Size too strong, or job left standing too long. | | *Trim edges with razor blade.* |
| **Mistake or imperfect stroke.** | | | *Wash paint off with turps and cotton, wipe dry before proceeding.* |
| **Cloudy gild.** | Glass insufficiently cleaned. | *Obvious.* | *No remedy.* |
| | Size not clear. | *Clean pail and brush; Use distilled water.* | *Wash gild with warm water.* |
| | Omission of second gild. | | *Obvious.* |
| | Poor quality leaf. | *Obvious.* | *Wash gild with warm water.* |
| **Cracks or holes in gild.** | Poor gilding technique; insufficient patching. | *Obvious.* | *More patching.* |
| **Leaf slides on wet size.** | See page 22. | | |
| **Leaf crawls away from varnish centers or outlines.** | Common experience. | *Four drops detergent per pint of size.* | *Extra patching.* |
| **Leaf won't clean off.** | Size too strong. | | *Use Bon Ami.* |
| | Gild standing too long. | *See page 40, 41.* | |
| **Streaky matte centers with shiny spots on single gild jobs.** | Center varnish too dry. | *See page 51.* | *Bon Ami over varnish.* |

| Difficulty: | Cause: | Prevention: | Saving the job: |
|---|---|---|---|
| **Water size lifts varnish centers.** | Gilding too soon; also see page 62 for procedure when more than one line of lettering. Wrong varnish. | | |
| **On two-gild jobs, leaf in center picks up when backing up.** | Center varnish too wet. | *See page 84, 85.* | *Wait longer before backing.* |
| **Backing over centers cracks.** | Center varnish too wet; not enough varnish in paint. | *Obvious. See page 74 for procedure with damar centers.* | *Another coat of backing color.* |
| **Job peels after short time of service.** | New glass insufficiently cleaned. | *See page 13* | *No remedy.* |
| | Varnish coating not tough enough. | *See page 44.* | *Revarnish.* |
| | Windows washed too soon. | *See page 44, 85.* | *Revarnish.* |
| | Windows sweating. | *See page 44.* | *Revarnish; back up with aluminum leaf.* |
| | Windows cleaned with strong materials. | *See page 44.* | *Revarnish.* |
| **Varnish crawls on letters.** | Varnished too long after completion of job. | *Varnish same day or next day.* | *Wash with turps, then water. Or, varnish with Dulux.* |

# Appendix B
# Buyers' Guide/Supplies

For updated information refer to the trade magazines and *SIGNS of the Times'* annual "Buyers' Guide." Also, check local suppliers.

**Abalone:** Fine Gold Lettering

**Asphaltum:** S.S.S. Enterprises; many lumber and hardware concerns.

**Bon Ami:** Faultless Starch Co.

**Brushes:** Percy P. Baker; M. Grumbacher Inc.; A. Langnickel; Heinz Scharff.

**Bulletin enamel:** Chromatic Paint Corp.; Consumers Paint Factory, Inc.; Danacolors, Inc.; T. J. Ronan Paint Mfg.

**Burling burnisher:** "Wild Bill" and Company.

**Capsules, 00:** Dick Blick Co.; Rayco Paint Co.; your local drug store.

**Cotton:** Stearns & Foster Co. (Mountain Mist Brand).

**Damar varnish:** S.S.S. Enterprises, your local yard goods store.

**Ellipse tools:** Ovalcompass; S.S.S. Enterprises (Brunskill Ellipsograph).

**Embossing pre-mixed fluid:** "Wild Bill" and Co.

**Enamel, bulletin and lettering:** See bulletin enamel.

**Enam-L-Koat:** Best Buy Banner Co.

**Fibroseal varnish:** Commonwealth Varnish Co.

**Florence japan varnish:** Commonwealth Varnish Co.

**Gel medium:** M. Grumbacher Inc.; Martin F. Weber Co.

**Gold size:** Art Essentials of New York, Ltd.; Dick Blick Co.; Chromatic Paint Corp.; Commonwealth Varnish Co.; Rayco Paint Co.; T. J. Ronan Paint Mfg.

**Japan color:** Chromatic Paint Corp.; T. J. Ronan Paint Mfg.

**Japan drier:** Chromatic Paint Corp.; M. Grumbacher Inc.

**Japan varnish:** See name of varnish.

**Jars:** Rayco Paint Co.

**Kit cans:** Dick Blick Co.; Rayco Paint Co.

**Leaf:** Art Essentials of New York, Ltd.; Dick Blick Co.; The Durham Co.; Gold Leaf and Metallic Powders, Inc.; Sepp Leaf Products Inc.; M. Swift and Sons, Inc.; Wehrung and Billmeier Co.

**Lettering enamel:** See bulletin enamel.

**Liqui-Seal:** Consumers Paint Factory, Inc.

**Mahl stick:** Griffin Mfg.

**Mother-of-pearl:** Fine Gold Lettering

**Oil color:** Chromatic Paint Corp.; Danacolors, Inc.; Winsor & Newton.

**Oil size (slow):** See gold size.

**Overcoat clear varnish:** Chromatic Paint Corp.

**Pin vise:** Griffin Mfg.

**Prep-Sol:** E. I. Du Pont De Nemours & Co.

**Primers:** Chromatic Paint Corp.; Consumers Paint Factory; Danacolors, Inc.; E. I. Du Pont De Nemours & Co.; T. J. Ronan Paint Mfg.; X-I-M Products, Inc.

**Quick size:** See gold size.

**Razor blades:** American Safety Razor Company.

**Razor blade holder:** Fine Gold Lettering.

**Res-N-Gel:** See gel medium.

**Rubbing varnish:** Chromatic Paint Corp.; T. J. Ronan Paint Mfg.

**Size:** See gold size.

**Spar varnish:** see overcoat clear, no real spars known.

**Spinning varnish:** "Wild Bill" and Company.

**3812S Solvent:** E. I. Du Pont De Nemours & Co.

**Trichoroethane:** Cerbini Laboratories; some sign supply distributors.

**Venice japan varnish:** Commonwealth Varnish Co.

**Vinyl primer:** See Enam-L-Koat.

**Wood letters:** See primers.

**Wood stains:** Signlife Systems.

# Appendix C Buyers' Guide
# Suppliers and Manufacturers

For updated suppliers and manufacturers refer to the trade magazines and *SIGNS of the Times'* annual "Buyers' Guide." Also, check local suppliers.

| | |
|---|---|
| **Art Essentials of New York, Ltd.**<br>Three Cross Road<br>Suffern, NY 10901<br>914-368-1100<br>800-283-5323 | *Gilding supplies, gold leaf, paints, coatings* |
| **American Safety Razor Co.**<br>Staunton, VA (24401) | *Stainless steel razor blades* |
| **Barclay Leaf Imports, Inc.**<br>21 Wilson Terrace<br>Elizabeth, NJ 07208<br>908-353-5522 | *Gold leaf, gilding supplies* |
| **Chromatic Paint Corp.**<br>P.O. Box 690<br>Stony Point, NY 10980<br>800-431-7001 | *Paints, japan color, varnishes, sizes, oil colors* |
| **Commonwealth Varnish Co.**<br>Cecil E. Sanders<br>R.R. 1, Box 155<br>Greenfield, IN 46140 | *Varnish, gold size, coatings* |
| **Consumers Paint Factory, Inc.**<br>P.O. Box 6398<br>Gary, IN 46406<br>219-949-1684 | *Paints, coatings* |
| **Danacolors/Triangle Coatings**<br>1930 Fairway Dr.<br>San Leandro, CA 94577<br>415-895-8000 | *Paints, coatings,* |
| **Dick Blick Co.**<br>P.O. Box 1267<br>Galesburg, IL 61401<br>309-343-6181<br>800-447-8192 | *Gilding supplies, brushes, gold leaf, other supplies* |

| | |
|---|---|
| **The Durham Co.**<br>54 Woodland St.<br>Newburyport, MA 01950<br>508-465-3493 | *Gilding supplies* |
| **Faultless Starch Co.**<br>Kansas City, MO 64101 | *Bon Ami* |
| **Fine Gold Sign Co.**<br>**Esoteric Sign Supplies**<br>1644 Wilmington Blvd.<br>Wilmington, CA 90710<br>213-549-6622 | *Gilding supplies,*<br>*Mother of pearl,*<br>*Angel Gold, Abalone,*<br>*razor blade holder* |
| **Griffin Mfg. Co., Inc.**<br>P.O. Box 308<br>Webster, NY 14580<br>716-265-1991 | *Mahl stick, knives,*<br>*holders, perforating*<br>*wheels* |
| **M. Grumbacher, Inc.**<br>30 Englehard Dr.<br>Cranbury, NJ 08512<br>609-655-8282 | *Brushes, paints,*<br>*coatings* |
| **Quill-Hair & Ferrule, Ltd.**<br>P.O. Box 23927<br>Columbia, SC 29224<br>803-788-4499<br>800-421-7961 | *Gilding supplies,*<br>*Glass smalts,*<br>*brushes, coatings* |
| **Rayco Paint Co.**<br>2525 N. Laramie Ave.<br>Chicago, IL 60619<br>312-889-0500 | *Gilding supplies,*<br>*paint, brushes* |
| **T. J. Ronan Paint Corp.**<br>749 E. 135th Street<br>Bronx, NY 10454<br>212-262-1100 | *Paints, varnishes* |
| **Sepp Leaf Products Inc.**<br>381 Park Avenue South<br>New York, NY 10016<br>212-683-2840 | *Gold leaf,*<br>*gilding supplies*<br>*Video instruction* |
| **Signlife Systems**<br>162 N. Diamond Street<br>Mansfield, OH 44902 | *Wood stains,*<br>*varnishes* |

| | |
|---|---|
| **Spanjer Brothers, Inc.**<br>1160 North Howe Street<br>Chicago, IL 60610<br>312-664-2900 | *Wood letters,*<br>*other letters* |
| **M. Swift & Sons, Inc.**<br>P.O. Box 150<br>Hartford, CT 06141<br>203-522-1181 | *Gold leaf mfg.,*<br>*gilding supplies* |
| **Martin / F. Weber Co.**<br>Wayne & Windrim Aves.<br>Philadelphia, PA 19144 | *Res-N-Gel* |
| **Wehrung & Billmeier Co.**<br>1924 Eddy St.<br>Chicago, IL 60657<br>312-472-1544 | *Gold leaf* |

# NOTES

# Index

# Gold Leaf Techniques Addendum

Kent H. Smith

Although I completely rewrote this text as the third edition for 1986 publication, this 1992 printing of the third edition of **Gold Leaf Techniques** needs additional update. Since it is impractical to rewrite the entire text each printing, I have chosen to add this addendum to the end of the book, including information from the 1989 addendum. On the following pages, I will address gilding related issues which have been brought to my attention or which I have discovered. While this text was never expected to include all the techniques ever used in gilding signs, the rapid advancement of technology and an increasing desire for efficiency have precipitated some new and revitalized techniques.

**Computer-Assisted Gilding**

The advancement of computer technology has prompted questions about incorporating computer capability with the art of gilding. The most frequently asked question is whether vinyl letters can be used to back up gold on glass. While it is possible to back up with vinyl and the transfer tape can begin the clean-up process, some serious questions mus be considered. Gold leaf on glass has traditionally been known and sold as the ultimate in durability, but the long term durability of vinyl letter adhesive is relatively unknown. Further, many who have tried the vinyls for back-up rely upon the final varnish for protection against water intrusion. There are three problems with this application. First, the vinyl itself does not provide the protective ridge against water intrusion that backup paint provides. Once water seeps under the vinyl, the vinyl may actually trap it between itself and the gold to eventually break down the gelatin which holds the gold on the glass. The integrity and durability of the job relies upon the role of each successive coat of paint, and not just the final varnish.

Secondly, the vinyl repels, or has a weak bond, between itself and the paint or varnish film. The same reasons that one must use barrier coatings to enable use of enamels on vinyl banners apply to sealing over vinyl letters with varnish. Paints and varnishes simply do not adhere to vinyl, much less bond to the critical edge of the vinyl letter.

Thirdly, the phenomenon known as "adhesive creep" creates additional problems. The fine "hairs" of adhesive which creep from around the edges of an applied vinyl letter will not allow subsequent coats of paint or varnish to stick in those areas. This adhesive creep will leave a pointed, ragged edge around the letter which is more unsightly than a ragged edge produced by a heavy deposit of pounce powder.

There are some viable and time saving uses for computer technology in gilding. First and most obvious, is to make paper patterns with the computer to obtain a more accurate reference for hand lettering the back-up paint. Just as obvious, is to use the computer generated masking for surface sizing. The mask is applied as with other paints however the gold size can be worked out with the brush to be as level as possible. Unlike using enamels, gold size should be left to tack with the mask in place. The size is pliable enough to not break as enamel does during mask removal, while it will tend to flow out of shape if the mask is removed too early. Computers can also be used effectively to cut screen printing film for vertical printing back-up. Photo screen positives can also be cut with the computer and this type of screen seems to deposit an ink film which is more suitable for gold leaf clean-up. Another method which has be used in the past is the application of a mask direct on glass and gilding, then back-up through the mask. This has recently proven to be a less viable method using leaf, which I no longer recommend, however, it does work well using "Angel Gilding" *(see below)*. As with any procedure, new advancements should be tested thoroughly. One should always guard against the temptation of utilizing technology to such an extent as to bypass quality.

## Angel Gilding

Angel gilding is a liquid solution (aqua regia) process of depositing gold on glass. The procedure is the same as that for silvering mirrors and produces a perfect mirror-finish of gold. Angel gilding was used by the production houses just after the turn of the century for gilding multiple copies of the same artwork. It is also the preferred method of gilding uneven surfaces such as glue chipped or etched glass.

While it is possible to angel gild on location, the process is more easily accomplished in the shop. The highly reflective mirror finish is also too "perfect" for many applications where leaf gilding would be more appropriate. The process and chemical compounds were "lost" until their rediscovery in 1988 by RICK GLAWSON, FINE GOLD SIGN CO./ESOTERIC SIGN SUPPLIES in Wilmington, California *(listed in Appendix C)*. Contact the company directly for angel gilding kits with complete instructions.

## Screen Printing Back-Up

Screen printing back-up is frequently used to either accurately reproduce complicated or small inscriptions as well as multiple impressions. For job site applications, printing is done vertically and therefore a thorough knowledge of screen printing itself and vertical printing in particular, is necessary before attempting this method.

As a materials update for those familiar with screen printing, the favorite of many is the entire line of *Colonial Screen Ink 5800 Series Dekor Gloss Ink*, which is unique in providing a clean, hard edge suitable for gold leaf. Most colors work fine although some have had difficulty with blue bleeding through the gild. Dekor dries quickly, as little as ten to twenty minutes, and cleans up right away. Amazingly enough, the Dekor can be thinned with turpentine and/or high temp reducer/flow enhancer combinations to a brushing consistency. Hand lettering is easy with this mixture although dry time is often doubled, depending on reduction amount. In any case, clean up should take place as soon as possible, and subsequent coats of paint or varnish should be delayed one to two hours.

While long-term durability as a backing paint has not been sufficiently tested, the material has been around for many years with a good record for exterior exposures. It is far preferable to the often used neon blockout paint which has a poor durability, although japan colors have a record of being durable. An additional advantage is that water size does not crawl away from Dekor and therefore no detergent additive is needed.

As a related screen printing note, gold size can be applied using a screen for surface gilding. The mixture preferred is to use a combination of enamel ink and quick gold size. About one third volume of size is used so the mixture retains the heavy body necessary for printing. While this is a viable application method, durability is questionable for long term as indicated by the discussion on enamels in the section on gold sizes below.

## Varnish

Should I varnish, when should I varnish, and what should I use? For exterior surfaces, clears will not be as durable as the gold itself. Remember that true cooked resin spar varnish in water white clear has not been available for many years. For rough service such as on vehicles, a varnish is required. Moderately rough service will be well protected by *Overcoat Clear* (Chromatic). Since this material is an alkyd, it will get brittle in time and may flake or craze. Two years seems to be common before the clear needs service. The life of the varnish can be extended by periodic waxing with standard paste wax (not the type that cleans as it waxes as this removes some of the varnish). Waxing the surface often doubles the life of the varnish. For very rough service vehicles such as fire trucks, a clear coat of automotive two component (catalyzed) urethane is an answer. Since this material is extremely hazardous, application should only be done by those certified in its use.

Glass gilding should always be varnished to protect it from washing and condensation. The *Overcoat Clear* works very well in this second surface application with known life so far of six plus years. I recommend to my customers, maintenance every three years for safety and to notify us immediately when damage occurs. When put into the perspective of other annual maintenance procedures, this is usually acceptable to the customer.

A newer product worthy of mention is *Clear Acrylic Topcoat*, which is a pure acrylic and water clear. Superior durability and non-yellowing are significant advantages along with not having a sulfur based solvent to tarnish metal leaf. A disadvantage is that it cannot be exposed to harsh detergents, solvents or gasoline. Therefore, it should not be used on vehicles but rather for other areas where protection is needed. The performance of clear acrylic is superior to all but the two-component urethanes.

## Gold Size for Surface Gilding

Sizes for surface gilding have presented some difficult questions in recent years. Raw materials have changed which have forced manufacturers to seek alternate formulations or discontinue the product altogether. Environmental regulations have forced many to change formulas again and the net result is a product without a reliable durability history. We gilders must always be aware of the limited size of our industry which makes it difficult for any manufacturer to cater to our special needs. The only gold size with a known reliability that I am aware of is Lefranc. Although the company has changed ownership and distributorship in the last few years, the product is substantially the same.

Lefranc three hour size (quick size) is ready for gilding in one to three hours with an open time up to three hours, depending largely on humidity rather than temperature. The twelve hour size (slow oil size) is usually ready for gilding in ten to twelve hours, though it can be as long as eighteen hours. Generally, it has an open time of twelve to eighteen hours, but it can be as long as thirty-six to forty-eight hours. The French-language label is not a set of important instructions, it only describes the type and quality of the size.

Over the years, lettering enamel has been used as a gold size. Since the enamel is made with a resin which continues to cure with age, it is not suitable to adhere gold upon. Once the surface cures to full hardness, it will release much of the gold. Combining gold size with the enamel lessens this problem but is still a questionable mixture for long term. This also emphasizes the rule of using pictorial oil colors to tint size.

## Miscellaneous Tips

Gelatin capsules have been inconsistent in some cases and some manufacturers have discontinued them altogether. Alternate sources for gelatin are easy to establish. Before gelatin capsules, gilders used powdered gelatin. Since this is an uncooked product, add 1/8 teaspoon (or cover a dime with a single layer) to a pint of boiling water (this is where the old controversy arose over whether to boil size or not). Remove from heat and allow to cool enough to handle, then strain to remove undissolved particles. Extra fine silk screen cloth or women's hosiery works well as a strainer. This size should be worked warm as it will gel if allowed to cool completely.

A superior replacement for capsules is sheet gelatine, an absolutely pure form of gelatin. The sheet is pre-scored into diamond shapes, four of which are used in a pint of water. Prepare the same as capsules, see page thirteen.

With the variations in gelatin consistency, adding a hot wash when needed is a reasonable alternative to the basic process of water size gilding to avoid clouded gilds. (Note that what is often perceived as a cloud is merely a pattern of the beating leathers used to pound the gold into leaves. These will not disappear and can be detected early by inspecting the leaf in the book from the side. Though all leaf will have a pattern it should be very faint so that it will not be magnified by the size. The better gold beaters change leathers often and take care in their alloys to avoid this). Patterns are also often put into the gold by the gilder when cutting with a fingernail. To avoid scar lines which appear as matte finish, use a soft base and cut with a gilder's knife. A hot wash is done with heated size between the first and second gild and sometimes adding a hot wash of clear water after all gilding and patching is done.

A superior tool for holding small pieces of razor blade for trimming tight areas is the *X-Acto #3111 Super 1 Knife*. The vise action of the holder grips the small pieces of blade tighter than any previously recommended.

Backing up can be easier with a change in pounce powder color. Use white powder when you wear dark color clothes, black when you wear white or light colors. DICK BLICK has a very fine grain powder which leaves little build-up.

An improvement on the burnishing templates pictured on page 93 is to make them from clear acetate. Acetate makes it easier to register the lines.

Fairly large templates can be made, particularly if the acetate is stretched on a frame in the same way as a silk screen.

New gilders tips can be prepared for use by applying a small amount of Vaseline hair tonic or Vaseline. Lightly pull the hairs between your fingers with a small amount of Vaseline on them. This type of charging can preclude stroking the tip in your hair and often will allow gilding as much as a full book of gold per charge.

*Ti-cote* and *WP1007* (Chromatic Paint Corp.) are superior barrier coats for vinyls and similar porous surfaces and produces an excellent substrate for gilding. Also available from Chromatic is *Chromaflo*, a flow extender which does not contaminate the gild and can be used in Dekor, japans and enamels. Their *High Temp Reducer* is a retarder which slows drying and makes paints more brushable. Blending cream can be used with japans to achieve soft transitions of color in shades and pictorial work on glass.

A superior adhesive to use with smalt in place of white lead or titanium is *Hold-fast Oil* from Byrne Sign Supply of Cleveland, OH or screen printers flock adhesive. These clear liquids have superior holding power and are to be used over color backgrounds the same as the color of the smalt. Colored glass smalts is available again from Quill-Hair & Ferrule.

Some caution should be used in making selections from the many types of gold leaf available on the market today. Some types are made for picture frame gilding or other ornaments, not signs. Some leaf contain alloys which make them unsuitable for use on varnish size or for exterior exposure as they will tarnish or corrode. Color changes and tarnishing can occur even if the leaf is sealed with varnish. Some leaves are heavy or contain alloys which make them unsuitable for water size gilding on glass. Take the time to be certain the leaf used is suited for signs. The better quality leaf will ensure a better quality sign.

Video instruction has been a practical way to get visual instruction with the ability to rerun as often as needed. I have two instructional videos available, *"Gold Leaf Basics"* and *"Intermediate-Advanced"* sponsored and distributed by Sepp Leaf Products and available from Signs of the Times and many fine distributors. They are priced individually with a special price for purchasing the two together, and were created as an educational service.

It is impossible to guarantee all of the methods suggested herein. There are too many variables such as climate, variations in basic materials from brand to brand and from batch to batch, surface differences in finish, texture and composition, as well as differences in individual abilities and techniques. It is assumed that once basic processes are learned, everyone will experiment and keep up to date with any new advancement.